Momma's Enchanted Supper

Momma's Enchanted Supper
and other stories for the long evenings of Advent

A Memoir
Carol DeChant

Loyola Press
Chicago

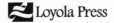 Loyola Press

3441 North Ashland Avenue
Chicago, Illinois 60657

"The Fang Club" appeared in a shorter form in *The Critic*. A small segment of "When Wisdom Spoke and We Saw Her Beauty" originally appeared in and was syndicated by the *Chicago Tribune*. "Grandma Says Yes" appeared in a shorter form in the *Chicago Sun-Times*.

Photo credits: p. 50—courtesy Kraft Foods; p. 80—courtesy Babe Didrickson Zaharias Foundation; p. 104—courtesy Israel Government Tourist Office, Midwest Region; p. 164—Richard Horodner, the Hurricane Photographer

Interior design by Leonard Telesca

Library of Congress Cataloging-in-Publication Data
DeChant, Carol.
   Momma's enchanted supper and other stories for the long evenings
of Advent/Carol DeChant.
      p. cm.
   Includes bibliographical references.
   ISBN 0-8294-1272-7 (hardcover)
   1. Advent—Meditations. I. Title.
BX2170.A4D43   1999
242'.332—dc21   98-56192
                                                                      CIP

Printed in the United States of America

99 00 01 02 03 / 10 9 8 7 6 5 4 3 2 1

Contents

To the Reader

As both an adoptive and birth mother, I'm suspicious of conclusions about families based on genealogy charts. Bloodlines charted as if people were trees may provide a helpful medical history, but they can't tell us who we are. That is the province of our stories. We are our stories, even when they're about others. We are the stories we cherish, the ones we repeat as well as the ones we fear and conceal. The stories we tell are responses to the ones we've heard before. Our stories form us, and many of them outlast us.

This book grew out of my observations about how we bring our own histories to the Bible. Interpretation of Bible stories depends upon where—and with whom—our sympathies lie. Biblical tales of exile and returning home, scorned or empowered women, sibling rivalries, parental favoritism, the mistreatment of or compassion for the afflicted—all are influenced by what has happened in our lives; often by our gender, birth order, or social status; and always by the stories retold in our families through the generations. Viewing Scripture through the lens of our personal history keeps the Bible everlastingly rich and fascinating, for we are always bringing new experience, questions, and understanding to the reading.

Each Advent day in this book begins with a brief quotation from one of the recommended Scripture readings for that date. It is followed by story-and-reflection related to the quotation in three parts: a personal or family history, an italicized meditation linking the biblical quote with my story, and a final "what happened," my own conclusion to the tale or theme. This format reflects the way the Bible can trigger a memory of our own stories, how one tale can become joined to the other, and even questions that may be asked as we try to make sense of both.

I hope to trigger the same experience in you. Stories of the adventures and misadventures of my ancestors should remind you of turning points in your own family life. A tale of my teacher may bring to mind one who encouraged (or plagued) you; our family's quirks and enduring values can evoke thoughts of how you have benefited from and what you have had to overcome in your heritage and what you hope to pass on. Dramatists claim there are only a few basic plotlines; all else is detail. It is these basics that unite us. As sons and daughters you and I are more profoundly linked by family than we may be separated by ethnicity, race, religion, culture, age, or politics.

These stories are tidier in the telling than they were in the living, where they were played out amid the morass of so many other concerns and activities. Hindsight imposes themes and patterns that reflect the teller's intentions as well as her characters' behavior. I compiled this book by reading my ancestors' written accounts, by researching relevant times and events, by questioning those who might remember and shed light, and by consulting my own memories (probably my most fallible source). Choosing what to tell and what to leave out is a highly subjective exercise. I confess I would have drawn different lessons from some of these anecdotes at earlier stages of my life. The years have influenced what I now see and emphasize. Given these realities, I have tried to tell the truth, to refrain from inserting unverified material to make the events or people easier to understand or like, and to edit only for clarity. In a few instances, pseudonyms have been used to protect the privacy of individuals.

This collection reveals lives filled with unexpected love and loss, with out-of-the-blue nastiness at times, and with meteoric kindness often. When I juxtaposed my family's stories against ancient Advent Scriptures, I found cycles of mystery and miracles; of a yearning to strike out for new territory and a persistent longing for home; of hoping and grieving, then daring to hope again.

Because Advent looks to past struggles while calling us to a grace-filled future, I also saw generations of mothers, fathers, daughters, and sons trying to get to the stable. Wishing to ask the Child not only "Who are you?" but also "Who am I?" and "Why am I here?" I find evidence that God can be Connector, as well as Creator-Sustainer-Redeemer, and that the Spirit abides in the time and spaces between our lives and events, as well as within us.

I hope these pages will encourage you to see that the stories you harbor in attics, scrapbooks, and memory are no less sacred than the ones contained in your Bible. Your tales and the ancient ones can expand and enhance one another. Reflect on your own stories, keep telling them to future generations, preserve their magic and their truth.

Carol DeChant

Chicago, September 1998

Acknowledgments

I am especially indebted to those who have been significant influences on my hopes and thoughts, leading to publication of this volume: LaVonne Neff at Loyola Press, Sister Marie Vandenbergh at Chicago's Cenacle, and the Reverend Greg Comella in Berkeley, California.

I am grateful to Michael McColly, Jack Dierks, my sister Harriett Harrow and her husband, Paul MacLean, for reading this manuscript and offering valuable suggestions, and to others who did the same for much of the book: Florida writers' groups led by Noreen Wald in Pompano Beach and Abe Cohen in Delray Beach; Sandy Wisenberg's class at the Oak Park (Illinois) Public Library; Cheryl Chaffin and her class at Chicago's Newberry Library.

I have been influenced by more writers and their work than I can name here, but those especially valuable for this book include Sally Cunneen's insightful *In Search of Mary* (Ballantine Books); Kevin Quast's *Reading the Gospel of John* (Paulist Press); Martin Buber; Frederick Buechner; Rabbi Abraham Heschel, especially *The Prophets* (Harper Torchbooks) and his essays in *Moral Grandeur and Spiritual Audacity,* edited by Susannah Heschel (Noonday Press); Rosemary Haughton; Hans Kung's *On Being a Christian,* translated by John Bowden (Image Books); John Leax; John P. Meier's *The Vision of Matthew* (Crossroad) and his two-volume *The Marginal Jew* (Doubleday); and Walter Farrell's four-volume *A Companion to the Summa* (Sheed and Ward).

A few years ago I discovered Alfred Delp, a German Jesuit who wrote about hope while he awaited execution by the Nazis. His essays made me want to write this book. Delp's timeless inspiration appears in English in *When the Time Was Fulfilled: On Advent and Christmas* (Plough Publishing; call 800-521-8011) along with pieces by Eberhard Arnold and Emmy Arnold, founders of the Bruderhof, a pacifist Christian community. That book deserves a wide audience.

My business partner of fifteen years, Kelly Hughes, graciously allowed me to take time for this project and helped me with research.

Without my family this book would not have been written; many are recognized in the following pages. My children, their spouses, and my grandchildren—who are still in the first acts of their own stories—have also encouraged and heartened me: Elizabeth, Matthew, and Jacob Bernier, and young David DeChant; Meredith and David Ashby; Brian and Arlene Anest DeChant; "Big" David and Ann Marie Wilson DeChant; Deborah Reinisch; Linda Reinisch, Al Twanmo, Isabel Caro Mai Twanmo, and Cecilia Caro Soong Twanmo.

My husband, Stanford Reinisch, allowed me the luxury of taking time off from my "regular" job to write. Thank you,

Stan, for occupying yourself with solitary pursuits for all those weekends and evenings, for not even counting how many there were, and for being my cheerleader, sounding board, editor, and inspiration.

The Hopes and Fears of All the Years

I got the camera, so I took this photo of Momma, Daddy, Harriett, and Kathleen on Christmas morning.

First Sunday

For family and friends I say,
"May peace be yours."

—*Psalm 122:8*

I have often tried to figure out just when I stopped enjoying Christmas and started dealing with it. When did the women in my family first become haunted by the Christmases That Once Were and the Christmases That Might Have Been?

Did it begin with the Divorced Christmases? Or earlier, when I became the parent generation and tried to make Christmas magic in a new town with no relatives nearby? Or does it go all the way back to when Grandpa and Grandma Miller stopped hosting Christmas because they were too old and tired and the grandchildren's families were too big and scattered? Then Grandpa Miller died on Christmas Day 1966, and the holiday came to signal the end of an era.

For many years, Christmas tended to irritate a scab called memory, tempting me to pick at it until I became infected with sorrow and dissatisfaction. I started going to Florida for the holidays, where even the Salvation Army bell ringers wear sandals and there are fewer reminders of Christmas as it once was. I found I was not alone: Florida radio stations limit the number of carols played during the season because so many listeners complain that Christmas music depresses them. In this frame of mind, even memories of childhood's happy holidays became a bittersweet measuring stick.

I think of my sister Kathleen crawling out of the top bunk, tiptoeing to the window, and shushing me to listen for reindeer on the roof. Isn't this the end of a perfect Christmas Eve?

It begins with Momma singing, "Over the river and through the woods to Grandmother's house we go" and laughing because we're going in the DeSoto rather than in a sleigh. Our grandparents' living room is filled with El Producto smoke and the din of everyone shouting, trying to top each other with Harry Truman stories. Daddy and Uncle Herb, who both married into this noisy clan, never raise their voices and never fully understand people who get such enjoyment from what sounds just like quarreling.

All of these Midwestern Democrats are wild about Harry, who really gave that music critic what for when he panned Margaret's singing. "Did you hear what Bess said," Grandpa hollers, spilling ashes onto the carpet, "when that reporter asked wasn't she embarrassed that Harry said 'manure' in his speech instead of 'fertilizer'?" And several voices laugh and shout Bess's reply: "No, I was relieved! Because 'manure' was better than what Harry usually calls it."

Aunt Hilda's jellied candies with powdered sugar are passed around, along with Momma's divinity and Aunt Betsy's fudge. Kathleen and I sit by the tree with our little sister, Harriett, eager to be asked to help pass out the gifts. I remember it as a time when we believed and hoped. I remember a season only of joy and contentment. But then, I remember hearing those reindeer hooves on the roof too.

As they journey to God's holy mountain, relatives and friends help the psalmist find peace and grant it to others. Everyone is invited to join them in honoring even the prospect of the celebration to come. Hopeful anticipation is heightened by memories of loss and disappointment. The movement through Jerusalem's gates and up the mountain inspires gratitude and generosity, a hope for peace on earth and goodwill towards others. The psalmist's family knows that much of life is an attempt to survive a chaotic, often hostile world, but they have also discovered that peace flourishes where love reigns. Good times with friends and family are cherished because they were once unavailable and endangered, feared to be extinct. They carry the hopes and fears of all those years up that mountain, provisions necessary to their enjoyment and appreciation of the ritual.

To people who have felt abandoned but now find God in their midst, a joyful celebration is serious business.

I have come to enjoy Christmas again. The psalmist is right: gratitude for friends and relatives brings me peace.

It also helps to laugh, observing that my Jewish stepdaughters are more sentimental about Christmas than any of us Christians. For Debbie, the holiday season is *It's a Wonderful Life, Miracle on 34th Street,* and giving gifts to everyone she loves. For Linda, it's about being together. She brings her family from Maryland, offering to be head chef for Christmas dinner.

Allowing myself to be haunted by the Christmases That Once Were and the Christmases That Might Have Been finally seems a morbid indulgence as my Jewish stepdaughters celebrate the Sacrament of the Present Moment. Debbie and Linda are having more fun than I am.

And it helps to pull Advent out of our haunted Christmases Past and out of the relentless countdown towards Christmas Future ("Only thirty shopping days left!") and observe it as a season unto itself. If Christmas requires faith (the great "nevertheless . . ."), Advent offers hope (a small "but still . . ."). Renewed hope differs from first-time hope. Mature hope is hobbled, like Jacob after wrestling with God's angel, treading more carefully now but with a truer sense of direction.

Most of all, gratitude for blessings helps. Appreciation breeds awe and wonder as I review such holidays as the year when . . .

❖ my neighbors the Berardis added three foster children to their home, which already included their four children, and decided all the kids would get new bikes for Christmas. Nick, a moonlighting firefighter with little free time, began assembling the bikes in a garage weeks before Christmas. A steady stream of adult visitors dropped by the garage to see Nick's progress. On Christmas morning, it seemed as if the whole neighborhood squeezed into the Berardi living room to share the children's joy and to marvel at the lineup of one trike and six shiny new bikes, all adorned with enormous red bows.

❖ my sister-in-law Marianne hosted us for turkey with all the trimmings, and the power went out in Fort Lauderdale. She alerted her husband, Dick, to bring Chicago-style hot dogs when he flew in that day from O'Hare. They cooked wieners on a gas grill and served them to a ravenously hungry family. We lingered at the table, agreeing that Christmas dinner had never tasted so good. Suddenly, heat, light, and music simultaneously burst upon us as the power was restored. We were not sorry it had waited long enough for us to be grateful for hot dogs and chips by candlelight, surrounded by loved ones.

❖ my grandson Matt suggested we find a volunteer opportunity over Christmas. We helped distribute a hot meal and groceries to migrant farmworkers and their families. In the process, we met a dedicated group of elderly year-round Floridians who forge ties to their community and to each other through their creative efforts to know and serve their seasonal neighbors.

❖ the old song changed to "Over the Okeechobee River and through Alligator Alley to Grandmother's house we go" because I have become Grandmother. I now see the cycle of children coming and leaving, of birth and death, as part of the Christmas pageant. For many years now, my own Christmases have been enriched by my grown children's return, bringing the most important gift of themselves and those they love, increasing our fun and multiplying our blessings with the ultimate expression of hope: babies.

A Better Choice
of Troubles

The Graneys when Daddy was about nine.

First Monday

They shall beat their swords into plowshares
and their spears into pruning hooks.

—Isaiah 2:4

We three daughters often begged my parents to tell how they met. As children, we loved stories of the flapper era, when young girls radically altered themselves and their world: casting off the hobbled skirts and tight corsets their mothers had worn, bobbing their hair, and inventing daring new dances. And we liked the involvement of several caring aunts in the story. Momma and Daddy—Guinevere and Howard—seemed caught up in a grand design as spellbinding and ethereal as a spiderweb, one that, eventually, spun out us.

Guinevere's broken heart provided a dramatic beginning. A man she thought she'd marry visited his dad in Wyoming and—influenced by the old man—broke up with her when he returned. Her mother—Grandma Miller—wrote her sisters, and Momma went to California, where Aunt Stella, Aunt

Blanche, and Aunt Ernestine tried to divert and restore her. Just after she returned, Momma met Daddy.

As grown women, my sisters and I have an enlarged understanding of the September in 1929 when they met: Howard, a small-town Irish Catholic boy whose grandparents came to Iowa during the potato famine; Guinevere, a Des Moines girl of English-German heritage and Presbyterian parents.

In 1929 Americanism was commonly equated with being white and Protestant, and intolerance and turmoil threatened: nine blacks had been lynched the prior year; increased immigration had led to antiforeigner outbursts; Irish Democrat Alfred E. Smith's nomination for president had unleashed anti-Catholic bigotry; a revived Ku Klux Klan had mushroomed.

Protestants and Catholics viewed one another as fundamentally, irreconcilably different. The prospect of the "other" infiltrating "our" loved one's affections terrified parents and clergy. Both sides preached against a mixed courtship, for it could lead to one's "conversion," causing a loss to his or her parents akin to death. A Protestant bride or groom was pressured to vow to raise the children Catholic; Catholic parents were expected to disown a child who married outside the Church and to refuse to attend the wedding.

When my parents told the story, this background was downplayed, as if being young and in Iowa offered a lovely, protective cocoon. But when pressed, Momma admits that dear family friends, "Uncle" Frank and "Aunt" Etta, refused to come to the wedding because it was in a Catholic church. "But they eventually came around," Momma adds. "Years later, your father did surgery on both of them."

She changes the subject: "Above all, there was dancing. You could go to a dance every night of the week in Des Moines. At the Cotillion, Hoyt Sherman Place, ballrooms." At home, she and her friend Lucia wore out the carpet in front of the mirror doing the Charleston.

And don't forget the aunts. Howard and his friend Don had come from Perry, Iowa, to Des Moines to study at Still Osteopathic College. Don, an orphan, had been raised by a Catholic aunt and sent to parochial school. Catholic and public school students never mixed in Perry. Don and Howard had never dated a Protestant girl or even become acquainted with one. In Des Moines, they roomed at the home of Don's aunt Lillian. This aunt, who attended the Presbyterian church with Guinevere's family, called Guinevere's mother to arrange blind dates. "Lillian told her about these two nice fellows who didn't know any girls in the city—protective like a mother hen over her chicks," Momma says. "I agreed to get Lucia and go to their college dance.

"Then your father phoned, and I asked, 'How tall are you? I'm tall for a girl,' and he passed the first test by saying he was six feet." She wanted to look good on the dance floor.

Guinevere was upstairs when Howard arrived. ("Still getting ready," she claims. "So she could make a grand entrance," he says.) Guinevere's mother went up to tell her "he seemed to be a nice boy, but much older than me. Ha! Looks deceive." She is older, by fifteen months.

How did our four grandparents surmount the prejudice of their day to welcome the "other" their child married? I ask. Momma reminds me that her parents had left the Seventh-day Adventist Church, and they didn't consider Presbyterian-to-Catholic as drastic as their own conversion. I remember being told in parochial school that I'd sin (by "causing scandal") if I went to church with my Presbyterian grandparents. I'd once asked Grandma Miller if she'd been sad when Momma became a Catholic. She'd said no, explaining that Presbyterians and Catholics share the same Apostles' Creed—a secret the nuns had been keeping from me.

My sisters and I were thankful for this family harmony, especially after we learned that, historically, my parents' ethnic-religious mix has meant war, such as the Troubles in Northern Ireland. Fortunately, Momma and Daddy and their parents considered marriage a better choice of "troubles."

Would Christ have inaugurated a church to splinter into sects and then persecute other believers with inquisitions, crusades, and wars? Did Christ intend to start a new religion? Or was he just trying to be a good Jew?

Whatever his intention, Jesus was an observant Jew influenced by Isaiah. He first preached from Isaiah's prophecy, according to Luke (4:18).

No doubt Christ, who told us to love our enemies, appreciated Isaiah's call to transcend our human nature and fulfill our deepest longing: to turn weapons of destruction into tools of nurture, swords into plowshares. Isaiah's challenge offers an abiding image: bury your hatchet in the soil—exchange carnage for sustenance.

If Jesus did mean to launch a religion, his followers often abort his mission. Irish Catholics and pro-British Protestants have slaughtered and terrorized each other for centuries. A peace treaty, affirmed on Good Friday amid assassination threats, has weary citizens daring to hope that neighbors who speak the same language, have the same skin color, and consider themselves followers of Christ can put aside their tradition of hatred and violence to live together. Yet after all these years, disarming hostility seems a more terrifying process than fostering hatred.

Is God concerned with religion or repulsed by it? How does the Prince of Peace endure the "troubles" we know in India, Northern Ireland, Nigeria, Bosnia, and—of all places—Israel?

Marriage is never without troubles. Momma and Daddy have often made me think of the words to an old song: "You might have been a headache, but you never were a bore." Their differences are in personality, though, not beliefs and values.

Subsequent generations' marriages have yielded a rainbow of national origins, as well as Catholics, Protestants, Jews, and those who don't define themselves with religious labels; homosexual and heterosexual persons; and adopted and biological children—but those are other people's classifications.

In families, there is no "other."

Not that the Catholic Graneys and the Presbyterian Millers weren't polar opposites in temperament and approach to life.

The Graneys are a people of few words, soft-spoken, good listeners who inspire trust. Daddy's sister Harriett, a quintessential Graney, was standing in line at a crowded post office when a man—a total stranger—picked her as the one to approach with "I feel sick." With typical self-effacing Graney humor, she told this story later, laughing, "Why me?" We knew why her: that I'll-make-everything-better aura the Graneys emit, so highly visible on the radar screens of the sick and needy. They're drawn to serving others, healing, teaching, and enforcing the law.

Momma's side, the Millers, are loudly talkative, funny, impatient, and easily upset. Especially when they're mustering a good tantrum and a Graney says, "Calm down." They're drawn to expressing themselves flamboyantly or to jobs where they can talk: the arts, public relations, millinery. Unemployed Millers write fiery letters to the editor and call radio talk shows.

Grandpa Miller, a nonstop talker, read aloud every billboard and street sign while driving. Grandma said she wouldn't marry him if he became a minister, which they both saw as a talking, rather than a serving, profession. So he memorized enough to pass the bar exam back when you didn't have to go to law school to take it. An attorney once told the court that his opposing lawyer, Grandpa Miller, had "verbal diarrhea," drawing delighted titters from the jury and spectators.

"I prefer verbal diarrhea to my opponent's constipation of thought," Grandpa shouted, eliciting hoots and applause.

A Graney would *tsktsk* (nonconfrontationally) to see a frustrated Grandpa Miller kick his unreliable car. Graneys think kicking tires accomplishes nothing at best, and at worst, it's probably not good for them. Millers don't indulge in long-range thinking or speculating on consequences; they leap to the instant therapeutic value of giving their Goodyears what for. Still driving at age eighty-seven, Daddy has never had a ticket, not even for a parking violation. Millers are back- and front-seat drivers who dispute their tickets as they're being written up and in court.

Momma once jumped up in a crowded theater—during the show—and screamed at the elderly man next to her, "You'd better *move*. Now!" As the old man shuffled up the aisle, she yelled to the amazed onlookers, "That damned fool pinched me." A Graney would have moved herself—quietly. Hearing the story, my Miller cousin Geraldine offered a third possibility: "When that happened to me, I said, 'Sir, I'll give you just twenty-four hours to get your hand off my knee.'"

Graneys are prone to cancer, alcoholism, and depression. Millers are prone to migraine, "gall bladder stomach," depression, and fainting (in church and near needles). My sister Harriett once fainted in the confessional. She came to with the priest silhouetted in the open door of her confessional. She doesn't recall any penance, other than several people—others waiting in line to confess—staring at her. She imagined them speculating on the sins she'd confessed as she blacked out. Harriett quit going to church, becoming—literally—a fallen-away Catholic.

Yet opposites attract. Grandma Miller once told me that many misguided Protestant friends offered their condolences on the "loss" of her daughter by the marriage. "Can you imagine?" Grandma scoffed, shaking her head at their blindness to her good fortune in getting Howard as a son-in-law. After they were long deceased, I told Daddy that I recalled Grandpa and Grandma Miller as the finest Christians I'd ever known. "Were they really that good," I asked, "or am I overlooking some flaws?" "No, they were as you remember them," he replied.

My parents don't see their marriage as a brave choice in 1930s America, when "others" were demonized. Momma admits that she feared the KKK and that her north-side neighborhood was a Klan stronghold then. "So wasn't the two families' acceptance a miracle?" I ask, recalling that both families were devout and active members of their churches.

But Momma recalls other details of seventy years ago: "We took the streetcar to the big ballroom downtown. Every Monday—'Ladies Free Night.' Took the last car back at midnight."

It's dinnertime at their retirement home, but I want to hold on to my wonderment: "But weren't our grandparents the most amazing part of the whole story?"

Daddy smiles in agreement as he helps Momma to her aluminum walker. She glides carefully across the floor. "Dancing," Momma says, preserving her own magic. "I used to say we'd always dance. I didn't think we'd ever stop dancing."

The Fang Club

*Our eighth-grade class with Monsignor Hansen,
during the only time we stood still and
behaved ourselves all year.*

FIRST TUESDAY

He shall strike the ruthless with the rod of his mouth,
*   and with the breath of his lips he shall slay the wicked.*
Justice shall be the band around his waist,
*   and faithfulness a belt upon his hips.*
Then the wolf shall be a guest of the lamb,
*   and the leopard shall lie down with the kid;*
The calf and the young lion shall browse together,
*   with a little child to guide them.*

—Isaiah 11:4–6

Eighth grade was the year we quit reading *American Girl* and started reading EC horror comics, a short-lived brand that offended our parents with graphic depictions of bloodsucking vampires and flesh-eating werewolves. It was the year I grew taller than my mother, gaining new power to defy the adults by sheer height and by the rebellion that seemed to be in the air. It was the era when Senator McCarthy raised bullying to new levels by ferreting out the Commies in our government, our colleges, and our movies.

It was also the year of the Fang Club, a year that still requires pseudonyms: for our nun, Sister Mary Agnes, to whom we were cruel; and for our class bully, Horencio, who taught us all we ever needed to know about power and its abuse. Sister Agnes (we called her "Aggie" behind her back) had just taken her vows; she was new in Des Moines and new at teaching. Most new nuns needed only their formidable black habits for authority. At Visitation School in 1952 that wasn't nearly enough for Aggie.

Not that any of us had it easy. Catholic children were burdened with special worries: Am I praying enough to get my grandparents out of purgatory? Will I die with mortal sin on my soul and roast in hell? If someone threatens to torture me unless I spit on the crucifix, what would I do?

Our real and present danger that year, however, was Horencio, a maniacal kid who was both class clown and class bully. Horencio was sixteen and still in eighth grade because he'd flunked. Everyone said that Monsignor Hansen had promised Horencio's mother that our school would accept him after the public school expelled him. *(That* was a switch!) We wondered if that bargain had something to do with all the tuition their family paid. They had ten kids, though none of the others were problems. Monsignor still got the worst of the deal. The adults had been had. Horencio, huge even for sixteen, spilled over his wooden school desk. Unable to sit still or be quiet, he'd have sudden, scary outbursts. Sometimes his grossly funny antics would end in a shocking finale— like the time he jumped up, walked around the room with his eyelids turned inside out, got the whole room laughing, then rammed his fist through a window. The rest of us, at thirteen, were scared, not just because of his power over us. We noticed that he also intimidated Aggie. We were stunned.

The Fang Club started that spring. I don't remember who Horencio bit first, but I'm sure we never wondered why. It would have been a typical burst of Horencio's nasty energy. Being bitten—long and hard—by Horencio made you a Fang Club member. Then you had to help jump on and hold down the next unwilling initiate while Horencio bit. His victims' arms carried the evidence for weeks. The skin around the teeth marks turned blue-green and began to peel. Everyone wore long sleeves to hide the bite mark. In eighth grade, the only thing worse than being initiated into the Fang Club was being the one who let the adults find out about it.

When Horencio decided to take a new member, he'd spread the word: "We're getting Daniel Harrington tonight." Then James DeBartolo. Conrad Byrd. Sometimes Horencio lied about who it would be. So whether you were the rumored prey or not, you'd spend the day frantically trying to plot an after-school escape. By the 3:10 P.M. dismissal bell you were mired in a sickening, sweaty hopelessness.

There were eighteen students in our class. As new Fang Club members were taken, those of us who were spared suffered a guilty relief and a growing dread. It was no longer just revulsion at Horencio's bite; it was the fear of his menacing pack. No one was surprised that our classmates would attack anyone Horencio pointed to. What was even more horrifying was that, once initiated forcefully, each new member seemed to *enjoy* being part of the next assaults. We were becoming a whole class of Horencios.

It ended suddenly. Thomas Bennigan's dad discovered his bite mark and made him tell. Poor Tom got the stool-pigeon stigma; the rest of us were secretly relieved. Horencio was never punished as far as we knew, and his domination of the room—and of Aggie—continued. We couldn't comprehend Aggie's apparent denial of the situation. Why had the order of things turned inside out in her classroom? (What if you spit on the crucifix and they tortured you anyway?) The concept of a nun floundering, scared, and perhaps even homesick was beyond our ken.

For her part, Aggie knew the bridge we'd all crossed together. She still led us in daily prayer for the conversion of Russia and the release of Cardinal Mindszenty. But there was no urging us to save room on our seats for our guardian angels. That was baby stuff (and besides, hadn't *they* abandoned *us*?). Nor did she give us any of those nun maxims ("Every time a young lady whistles, the Blessed Mother cries"). Margaret Perkovitch stole cigarettes from her mother, and all of us girls had our first smoke right in the school john. Whistling was kindergarten-level rebellion; we were headed for high school.

After graduation we heard that Aggie had been sent back to her Chicago motherhouse. We were both ashamed of our role in what was whispered to be her "nervous breakdown" and excited by the power it lent us. When I was in high school, I heard that Horencio had been dishonorably discharged from the marines. I hoped that Aggie had heard: even the marines couldn't handle him.

Isaiah's vision of perfect peace is one in which humans attain fullness through the knowledge of God; an absence of war is just one result. His song of hope describes nature and humankind transformed: fear is banished because human hearts are changed. The wicked no longer prey on the weak.

This message is important to people who lived when the ancient bullies ruled: the infant-slaughtering Pharaoh and Herod; Goliath, who can't find anyone his own size to pick on even if he tries. But Paul is the biblical bully I know more fully: a vicious abuser, heady with the power gained from persecuting others. Just like me.

Paul's heart is changed on the road to Damascus, but his peace is not the absence of struggle. He suffers beatings with rods and lashes, a stoning, imprisonment, shipwrecks, and a perpetual "thorn in the flesh." He is ashamed to name it, even to his dearest friends in Christ. Epilepsy? Homosexuality? Stigmata? Whatever it is, it could result in Paul's being put to death if it becomes known.

Isaiah's peace is magnificently described in his paean to justice; Paul writes of his peace in the majestic first letter to the Corinthians. There is hope for us all.

Horencio was our real teacher that year. He revealed the bully in us all, how easy it is to become the abuser, even (especially!) as we fear being out of control.

Senator McCarthy's power dimmed, but not without inflicting great damage. Senator Kefauver's Crime Commission put EC comics out of business for contributing to juvenile delinquency, and the artists and writers went on to a new magazine called *Mad*.

I moved away after college, and my parents moved across town. We came together in a different house in a new part of town, and I brought my children.

It was almost twenty years before I went to Mass in the old parish again. There I saw Horencio cradling a baby as he walked up to receive communion. His pregnant wife followed, holding an older child by the hand. After Mass, I asked around.

Passing age thirty seemed to do it: Horencio had become just like the rest of us.

The Indelible Stain of Homesickness

*A menu featuring Dr. John's wellness diet,
which was served at the Kellogg Sanitarium when
Grandma was a young TB patient in the 1890s.*

FIRST WEDNESDAY

*The LORD is my shepherd; I shall not want. He maketh me
to lie down in green pastures: he leadeth me beside the still
waters. He restoreth my soul: he leadeth me in the paths of
righteousness for his name's sake. Yea, though I walk
through the valley of the shadow of death, I will fear no evil:
for thou art with me; thy rod and thy staff they comfort me.*
—Psalm 23:1–4 (KJV)

She was placed in a sanitarium in 1894 at age seventeen,
far from home, alone, sick, scared, desperately missing
her parents and three sisters. I was about twelve when Grandma Miller told me about her year in the sanitarium, about
the blue dresses the female patients wore. She cried so much,
wiping her eyes on the skirt of her dress, that a faded spot
marked where her tears had bleached out all of the color.

Almost twenty years before, tuberculosis had become the
leading cause of death in America. It was thought to have
begun among the Sioux, then spread to the Navajo. Later it
even invaded the arts with consumptive maidens and poetic
meditations on the death of the young. Ralph Waldo Emerson, who had it and lost his bride and two brothers to TB,
referred to his "house of pain"; it stalked Stephen Crane, who
would succumb to "the white plague" at age twenty-nine;

Henry David Thoreau, also afflicted, saw in fall's spotted maple leaves "decay and disease . . . like the hectic glow of consumption." America's physicians refused to believe in Europe's theory about the contagious nature of the disease; most, like the general public, saw it as an act of God.

As bad as tuberculosis was, it didn't cause Grandma's tears. "I had homesickness," she told me, "the worst sickness in the world."

I inherited the scrapbook Grandma made when she was in the sanitarium. Her name, Maud, is embroidered on the quilted cover. The inside pages, made of oilcloth, have ads for tonics and sewing machines and salt, along with inspirational cutouts: "The Lord is my light and my salvation" and "Yea, though I walk through the shadow of the valley of death, I shall have no fear." The illustrations are of smiling, rosy-cheeked children in Edenlike gardens. Home. I thought of that girl in her dark valley a century ago, wearing a tearstained dress, trying to preserve pictures of green pastures, images of home.

In these times, agribusiness, death, divorce, and downsizing swallow people's homes, along with their livelihoods in some cases. I kept Grandma's scrapbook with me during my tumultuous postdivorce years. She was right about homesickness, I discovered.

How does one stop mourning a home and a life that is gone?

Why does the Twenty-third Psalm—a song that seems to offer hope and confidence to Grandma and so many others—evoke tears? Why is this expression of gratitude for God's countless gifts most often recited at times of unbearable loss? Is there a lament beyond its words of thanksgiving, a longing beneath its praise, a shakiness behind its expressions of courage? Why does the dark valley seem so imminent; the green pastures and restful waters farther away, in a past or future time?

Did Grandma sense—as I do—that the psalmist encourages and fortifies himself in the process of thanksgiving? That if the psalmist is not in the midst of terrible times, he has been through them? That he has learned that one arrives at joy and hope only after one has traveled through desolation?

My sister Harriett discovered that divorce had left me like Lot's wife: looking back, paralyzed over a past in ruins. She sent a bizarre assignment from New Hampshire: "Write down what you want to be doing, feeling, thinking a year from now. Consider as much of your life as you can: where you want to be, what you want to be doing, thinking, even, maybe, what you want to be wearing. Put this all in an envelope, seal it, and date it one year in advance. Don't open it until that day." She didn't explain.

I kept the sealed envelope in a top drawer, where I saw it frequently. Within a short time, I could remember only a few things I'd written. As I worked to get the tools I needed for my livelihood, I no longer remembered anything I'd written on that paper. Those "goals" weren't important because I couldn't recall what they were. Getting through each day occupied my thoughts.

When I opened the envelope, I was surprised to discover that my fears of a year ago were beside the point in my life now. Most of my concerns then seemed confused or trivial, reflecting a struggle to even imagine moving on. Harriett had nudged me out of reliving my past and put me into a present that presumed a future even before I had the heart for one.

Grandma was with me, along with her scrapbook, during that time. When I couldn't see God's face, at least one from his communion of saints comforted me. By the end of the year, my image of her as a homesick girl faded, and my memory of the woman I had known was restored.

"It was peculiar," she'd say, grinning about the rigid minister she'd once known. "He forbade us to play cards, but he shouted from the pulpit, 'Sin is as black as the ace of spades!' Now how did he know the ace of spades was black?"

"Peculiar" was one of her favorite words, along with "sanctimonious," "pretentious," and "persnickety." Grandma wrapped these words around the secrets she told grandchildren about how contradictory grown-ups could be. She recalled another "learned" minister with a string of degrees after his name who lifted his sermon anecdotes from *Reader's Digest* (to which most in his congregation subscribed). She laughed at dignified Mr. Harmon, whom Grandpa drove to work. Not realizing that Grandpa's usually filthy car had been washed, Mr. Harmon spit on the window he thought was open because he could finally see out of it.

In the kitchen, Grandma whistled, a habit considered vulgar in her youth. She recited the verse a sanctimonious teacher had used to warn her: "A whistling girl and a crowing hen will always come to a bad end." My sisters and I would smile, understanding Grandma's point that her teacher had mistaken "ladylike behavior" for actual womanly virtue. Grandma would get down to business, assigning each of us a different colored batter—red, green, yellow, and she'd take the chocolate—for her dazzling marble cake, saying, "Many hands make work light." But the lightness of being in Grandma's kitchen transcended the work there, and cooking became an incidental lesson.

The cheerful Grandma I had known—once restored in my memory—consoled me, and my image of the girl in the tearstained dress faded. I realized the scrapbook had helped her cope with homesickness, just as it—along with Harriett's "future" exercise—helped me hold on to my notion of home.

When I think of Grandma's tearstained dress, I wonder why we forget the sharp pains of childbirth, though memories of the dull ache of homesickness, once experienced, can be evoked forever after.

Daddy claims that certain "what will become of me?" fears stay with you always, even when the worst you dread never happens. The memory of that fear may govern all your actions for the rest of your life. The Great Depression did that to his generation. "When you're in it, you don't know it'll ever end" is his explanation for that fear's staying power. Homesickness and divorce evoke that kind of fear.

So the shadow of that peculiar sadness follows you, that longing for the way things once were, that search for a safe haven, a time and place where you belonged. It's there, planting the seeds of empathy and wisdom to grow within you. It lingers so you will enjoy being grateful once you've rediscovered your capacity for happiness. After you've reclaimed the psalmist's hope that goodness and kindness will follow you, too, all the days of your life.

Why Nuns Don't Have Wrinkles

Momma loves hats, and this stovepipe with feathers and paisley-patterned veil is one of her all-time great ones.

FIRST THURSDAY

Everyone who listens to these words of mine and acts on them will be like a wise man who built his house on rock. The rain fell. . . . But it did not collapse.

—Matthew 7:24–25

Whenever we drove through the countryside, Momma would look out at a rolling patchwork pattern of crops in a dozen shades of green, all pushing up out of the coal black soil, and declare it beautiful. "I'm an Iowa girl" is her way of telling you everything you need to know about her. She's referring to her heartland values: tolerance, a respect for learning and hard work, a lack of pretentiousness, and a belief that grit is developed by going against the grain.

My parents have been lifelong Democrats in a Republican state, though the independent Hawkeyes (commemorated in Mason City songwriter Meredith Wilson's "Iowa Stubborn") can also vote against their grain. In the sixties and seventies, my folks liked maverick Democratic governor and U.S. senator Harold Hughes, a recovering alcoholic who campaigned for liquor-by-the-drink in what was then a dry state in which you could buy only bottled alcoholic beverages for home consumption. Non-Iowans found him difficult to pigeonhole: a former truck driver of an evangelistic Protestant persuasion who was a dove on Vietnam. Hughes would call meetings to order by hollering, "All right, you sons of bitches, let's pray." Iowans considered him a man of practical integrity.

That brand of cognitive dissonance spills out of me once in a while in the form of Momma's maxims. Her pet phrases got molded into my gray matter early on. Whether I agree with the sentiments or not, they pop up like toast, to be passed out while they're hot and ready.

She has strong opinions on everything, but most of Momma's mantras concern food, child rearing, and education. Though she's in her late eighties now, when I envision her, Momma's in her thirties, wearing red slacks (her color—she was even married in a cranberry red velvet dress) and standing in our white-and-chrome kitchen with a fist planted on one hip, saying:

"Eat those bread crusts; they make your hair curly."

"Eat that burnt toast; it's good for your teeth."

"Honey is the perfect food."

"Never eat home-canned food. Whole congregations have been wiped out at church picnics, poisoned by home-canned food."

"The reason nuns have no wrinkles is *they have no children!*"

"My sister Elizabeth can cook and sew and she got a boy; I have no domestic talents and I got three girls."

"Mothers never think any girl is good enough for their sons; I'm glad I have only daughters."

"You girls were all toilet trained at seven months."

"Learning is never wasted."

"A woman needs a college education, just in case."

"No one can ever take your education away from you."

"I don't have a college education, but I know better than . . ." She would then cite a professional person's stupid remark in order to show that college doesn't instill wisdom or common sense.

"I always wanted to play the saxophone." This one was so frequent, I grew up believing that those missed music lessons had blighted Momma's life. It has only occurred to me as I write this that she could have taken sax lessons all those years she was pining for them.

Some of her sayings appeared contradictory. The most frequent dueling mottoes were "If there's anything I can't stand, it's a liar" and "The truth hurts." Momma portrayed truth as a damned-if-you-do-damned-if-you-don't virtue, but she made clear the necessity of telling it and taking the consequences.

Momma collected human disaster the way others saved stamps and salt and pepper shakers. She and Grandpa Miller kept abreast of the worst possible scenarios with subscriptions to *Official Detective* magazine. They enjoyed discussing each month's featured crime victims. When I worked as a camp counselor, Momma sent me clippings showing a serial killer's cabin in the Wisconsin woods where he'd skinned his victims to make lampshades. The gory scene was meant to discourage me from accepting rides into town on my days off: this was the type of person driving Midwestern highways.

Other people got letters filled with family news, weather, and local crop conditions. Momma reported sensational crimes from all over the country. Here is an excerpt from her letter to me on July 14, 1957:

"I'm enclosing a story out of August *Official Detective* about the murder of a 12-year-old boy. . . . It, as you will notice, happened while he was at Boy Scout Camp in Michigan, the camp run by the same Evanston Scout Offices you are employed by. . . . Two staff employees in that camp were sex deviates. . . . The handy-man who committed the crime also polished off another 14-year-old boy and two small girls. So travel in groups [though] you might also recall the three teen age boys in Chicago who were murdered and dumped, and they were in a group, so please do be very careful.

"Also, about the swimming. You know what causes most drownings. . . ."

She was ever thankful we were alive and well. When we were dealt setbacks, she reminded us things could have been worse (and provided lurid examples of how much worse). She would always point to someone—or a whole class of people—who coped with more obstacles in a day than we would probably encounter in a lifetime.

This sensitivity no doubt triggered her affinity for the underdog. After a priest told her unbaptized babies go to limbo—the suburbs of hell—she thought about all those holy innocents and called his doctrine hogwash. She moved us from a Catholic grammar school to a public high school because "you won't be living in a Catholic world." She felt, as Catholics in a Protestant land, we would sometimes be living in a hostile one. Our public high school's slogan, "Lee Township against the world," resonated with Momma's underdog views. (The girls' Catholic high school motto—translated from the Latin—"Lilies among the thorns," was "above it all" rather than underdogish.) When anti-Catholicism erupted throughout the country during John F. Kennedy's presidential campaign, Kathleen and I felt that old Joe, like Momma, had prepared his son to survive it: he'd sent him to Harvard instead of Notre Dame. To us, Harvard was a "public school."

Foundations are erected throughout childhood, subtly, unconsciously, and intentionally. They're built with words and with deeds and sometimes by failing to speak out or act. Christ's

lesson about building your house on a strong foundation is about
listening to his message and then doing his work. His house-
building metaphor concludes the Sermon on the Mount, a blue-
print for good works: Blessed are they who act mercifully, justly,
single-heartedly, and with pure motives. Forgive and love—
even your enemies. Don't use (abuse) the law to abandon your
wife, masking your immorality by appearing to be law-
abiding. Find preachers and teachers who speak truth, not ones
who (merely) speak glibly. Give alms privately; pray simply.

Sounds just like Momma, who would add, "Don't think
you're better than anyone else" and "Never eat potato salad
that's been out in the sun."

An almighty Solace, Sustainer, and Stronghold is a cozier
divinity than one who is Judge, but the biblical God is all of
these. You're being judged, Christ says, and the standard you
use to measure others will be used on you. How could it be other-
wise? Know this, and let the light of your good deeds shine before
God and humankind.

Judge Momma goes along with that, too, but she objects to
wrathful Armageddon scenarios. Perhaps that's why my sister
Harriett envisions an End Times in which the heavenly Accoun-
tant reviews the good deeds of our lifetime.

It all makes me wonder about the foundations I've erected:
Which of my words are imprinted on my children's minds for-
ever? What deeds will they remember me by?

Momma was the disciplinarian, the one who was home
with us most of the time. Daddy corrected me twice; "scold-
ed" is too harsh a word. He imparted lasting lessons simply
by revealing I'd let him down. In eighth grade, my friend
Sharon and I started calling our parents "the old man" and
"the old lady," though not to their faces. Once after we'd
been on the phone, Daddy took me aside to say he'd heard
me refer to Momma disrespectfully. Embarrassed, I dropped

those phrases from my repertoire of galling assertions of independence.

The other time we were riding in the car, listening to the radio. Mr. Bogey, a man who'd done odd jobs for our family for years, was also a Pentecostal minister. He suddenly came on the radio, giving a fiery sermon. My sisters and I were astounded at the transformation of the soft-spoken man into a raucous preacher shouting about Jesus. We giggled. Daddy snapped off the radio. "Have you ever considered what a non-Catholic walking into a Mass might think—hearing all that Latin mumbo jumbo?" he asked. "And how you'd feel if that non-Catholic made fun of *you*? Mr. Bogey is completely trustworthy. He is a good Christian." This brief Golden Rule lesson, softly spoken, is one that even Harriett, only seven then, remembers.

In two very different styles, my parents tried to teach us to walk in another's shoes, to see faith as a journey towards righteous living, to respect those who take different roads to that destination. Believing we've found the only true path means we've actually lost our way.

Khrushchev, Kennedy, and Aunt Harriett

*Aunt Harriett, a striking redhead with
blue-green Irish eyes, couldn't leave Iowa, so the
world came to her.*

First Friday

Families are comprised of those who leave and those who stay. Place—that landscape containing one's people and their stories—is essential to the well-being of those who stay. Familiarity breeds contentment. These are the kind of folk who drew ancient maps, writing "Here be monsters" in the unexplored territories. Thus warned, the leave-takers must balance their anxieties about unknown monsters with the excitement of finding something new.

Like most Americans, I romanticized leave-takers as a girl, thinking of those brave pioneers who established the colonies, then began the westward movement. I overlooked that staying requires courage too. Sometimes in greater measure.

Aunt Harriett stayed. As the youngest of five, it fell to her to care for her aging parents in the old family home built by her O'Malley grandparents. A soft-spoken, strikingly pretty redhead with blue-green Irish eyes, she was modest and kind. I assumed she never hesitated to stay in Perry, Iowa, to do what needed to be done. Her other siblings had families; some, like my father, had moved to the city. Being from the city (Des Moines), I didn't envy what I assumed was her dull life living with her parents in a small town.

It also seemed that her duty would extract the high price of spinsterhood, which in that day meant suffering the pity of the married. She turned thirty, then thirty-five, too busy and not of a nature for regrets. She did volunteer work for her town, her church, her country and opened her own insurance agency on the second floor of the big old house. She called clients who came after office hours "ghosts" because in the first-floor bedroom Mom and Dad Graney could hear the clients' footsteps overhead.

Harriett and her widowed sister, Martha, got boxer dogs from the same litter. The two tall women wore the styles of the forties well. I recall Harriett wearing those striking outfits into the early sixties: open-toed platform shoes, dresses with prominent shoulders, big picture hats over long hair that was upswept at the sides. Harriett and Martha walking Bosco and Bismark made a regal foursome.

As a teenager I began to revise my view of Aunt Harriett; listening to her stories made me realize how much she enjoyed her life. When an Arthur Murray studio opened, the sisters took dancing lessons, and the third floor of the old house was eventually turned into a ballroom. She and Martha smoked cigarettes from long slender holders, the way movie stars did. Bound to a town, a house, and a duty, Harriett seemed quietly confident that the world would come to her. It did.

Eugene McCarville moved to Perry in 1949 and rented a room at Great-Aunt Martha Spaulding's house. His first day in town he heard news of a terrible auto accident. That morning a farmer had found a woman who'd lain unconscious in his field all night in the rain. She was sent to the hospital in critical condition. Everyone spoke well of this woman, and the new man in town became curious. In time Harriett recovered, and Mac's landlords invited her to come play bridge and meet their new tenant. Recalling his first impression, Mac said, "I found a woman of unique presence and true humility. She was a lady from the heels up." They married, and Uncle Mac moved into the family home.

Unlike Aunt Harriett, Soviet premier Nikita Khrushchev was a leave-taker with global credentials. Our cold-war enemy launched *Sputnik* into space to demonstrate Soviet superiority to America and to the world. In 1959 he said yes to President Eisenhower's invitation—or dare—to come to America. A visit to the alien land of the monster capitalists was too enticing to refuse.

Khrushchev, a man with peasant roots, asked to see U.S. farmland, so the Roswell Garst farm outside of Perry was on his itinerary. In his memoir, *Khrushchev Remembers,* the Russian described Garst as "a capitalist, therefore one of my class enemies, but [one] I respected for his . . . willingness to share his experience . . . with us. Such capitalists are . . . a great rarity. . . . There are only two or three like him, but no more." The farm was extraordinary; the rich Iowa soil yielded unbelievable quantities of corn.

Everything was too impressive for the Soviet premier. He suspected he was being played for a fool, being led to believe that all Americans lived so well. The shrewd Russian had an idea: he would challenge the Americans to let him visit a home not on the official itinerary and see what he'd find behind those doors!

So that is how Nikita Khrushchev's security chief, General M. V. Zakharov, accompanied by translators and State Department officials, knocked on Aunt Harriett's door one summer day, an advance stop meant to assure security for Premier Khrushchev's visit to the home.

The Israelites are stayers. Being forced to leave, suffering exile, is the most tragic plight. The Promised Land is a goal, a dream of home; it is where we find God. Isaiah writes to a people whose identity and purpose are bound to their land. Jerusalem can be fortified, and peace is possible only by making a strong commitment to God, he says. Then we will be a righteous people. There will be no worry or want. The humble will be joyful, and the tyrant will no longer rule.

Jesus is a leave-taker, a misfit who doesn't marry or settle down, an itinerant without a place to lay his head. He always forces others to make the decision, saying, "Are you coming with me or not?" Christ pioneers a radical new kingdom open to prostitute and leper, tax collector and shepherd, Jew, Greek, Russian, and Iowan. The place where God dwells, he says, pointing to his heart, is right here within you.

Prophets are always dismissed. Even Jesus' relatives fear he is mentally unsound. Everyone assumes the superiority of the city, the greater credibility of the more worldly. Noting that Jesus keeps unsavory company and makes controversial claims, sophisticated people point to his unimpressive backcountry origins. Isn't he a carpenter, Mary's son? "Can anything good come from Nazareth?" Nathanael asks Philip (John 1:46). And the worldly-wise echo down through the ages:

Wasn't that man born in a log cabin in Kentucky?

Isn't he the son of that preacher from Ebenezer Baptist Church?

Isn't that tiny old woman in Calcutta an Albanian?

Could there be any merit in a lifetime spent in Perry, Iowa?

General Zakharov's report of what he found at Aunt Harriett's house discouraged Khrushchev's visit. I often imagine the security chief describing to the premier typical activities he may have seen there: "On the first floor were religious icons on the walls and photos of an old man, an old woman, and a dog—all dead now. They said that the old man used to finger prayer beads while reciting incantations, and the animal at his feet howled responses. The husband, wearing an apron, was making a chocolate-peanut-paste confection— 'fudge'—for many nieces and nephews. Upstairs, the wife conducted capitalistic transactions in a business office. And on the third floor, they put on music and invited me to dance in a ballroom!" That house wasn't "typical" enough for the premier, it was rightly decided. Or perhaps wrongly decided. Something good did come from Perry, Iowa: the Soviet secret service found Midwestern American values there.

The next year, Aunt Harriett, an Iowa delegate to the Democratic National Convention in Los Angeles, voted with the majority to nominate John Fitzgerald Kennedy as the nation's youngest and its first Catholic president. Two years later Harriett waited with the rest of the nation as Kennedy and Khrushchev went to the brink of nuclear war over Soviet missiles in Cuba, before Khrushchev backed down.

In 1964 Khrushchev was ousted from leadership, partly because of his unsuccessful agricultural policies. His memoir concludes with these words: "My only future is to go to the grave. I want to die. It is so dull—so dull and boring for me to live in my situation." He died in 1971 and was buried without a state funeral.

Uncle Mac was at Aunt Harriett's bedside when she died in 1989. Those who loved her sang "When Irish Eyes Are Smiling" as they carried her casket out of Saint Patrick's Church in Perry. She is buried in the little Iowa town where she had never once been bored.

The Very Best Kind of Brain Tumor

*The nurse's news to "Little Harriett" about her brain
tumor made us laugh until we cried.*

First Saturday

I may have been watching the O. J. Simpson trial—it was
omnipresent then and in our own ordeal to come—when
my sister Harriett called from Austin to say that her surgery
was scheduled for March in Los Angeles. She told the nurse
in L.A. that she had been surprised at the surgeon's speedy
reaction to seeing her MRIs. Her Texas physician's diagnostic process had been slow since she'd gone to him months
ago with a hearing loss. Harriett told me that the cheerful
nurse, sensing her alarm, said, "Don't worry, you have the
very best kind of brain tumor."

"Oh, goody. For a second I was worried," I said, and we
laughed. We favor black humor as a coping device; the ludicrous so often escorts the terrible.

Harriett is the kind of patient who becomes a lay expert
on her condition. While awaiting her doctor's consultations

with other specialists about the strange shadows on her MRIs, she'd gone right to work researching what might be wrong.

She began to suspect a brain tumor, a specter that evoked memories of our aunt Betsey's death thirty-five years earlier. By the time her doctor recommended a neurosurgeon, Harriett had already found one. His clinic specialized in operating on tumors of the eighth auditory nerve.

Harriett asked if I'd come to be there during the surgery. Her husband, Paul, of course, would be there too. They had married just three months before her diagnosis. I'd met him only once before their wedding, at a family party.

Patients' families got special rates at a hotel that provided transportation to the world-famous clinic. The hotel was near the courthouse holding the "Trial of the Century."

L.A. was even more obsessed with the trial than the rest of America. All three networks broadcast the trial there, along with Court TV and CNN. Every cabdriver gave you his theory of the crime while watching his portable TV as he navigated the freeways. Radio talk shows focused on minutia, confident that listeners knew every detail.

The night before surgery, Paul, Harriett, her daughter Hillary, and I ate dinner at the hotel restaurant. At a nearby table, two men sat with a woman whose head was wrapped in a scarf. Identifying the woman as a post-op patient, Harriett decided she had to speak to her. She approached the woman's table, saying, "Pardon me, I couldn't help but notice that you're obviously recovering from brain surgery." One of the men spoke with a heavy accent, and Harriett couldn't understand him. She addressed the woman again, pointing to her head. "You're doing so well. How long ago did you have your operation?" Harriett finally realized the woman's headdress reflected her caste or her religious beliefs, not brain surgery.

In the lobby where Harriett reported this exchange, we burst into laughter. So much for inspiration! Then we sat down to run through the next day's drill: her living will and the surgical procedure. Three doctors were needed: one would carve through her skull; another would remove the tumor with microsurgery; a third would remove fat from her stomach to use as a plug for brain fluid. Harriett made us promise to keep her awake while they shaved her head, to make sure they shaved the correct side. Sometimes the wrong leg has been amputated; you can't be too careful. I shuddered.

The next morning we were waiting for Harriett to go up to surgery when a nurse said Harriett's doctor in Austin had faxed the wrong records to the operating room. "Your surgeons are waiting for you to call Texas and straighten this out," the nurse said. Paul picked up the bedside phone, but the hospital switchboard gave him trouble about long distance. Fighting panic, I marched out to the nurses' station to protest. I couldn't find anyone to ask why the surgeons themselves didn't call the Texas doctor to clarify their needs.

Then a lab girl carried a tray into Harriett's room just as the Texas confusion got resolved. I rushed back to Harriett's bedside. In the countdown now, everyone was jittery. Except the lab girl. She reached over to the TV, flipped on the Simpson trial, then asked us to leave the room.

I stormed back to the nurses' station to demand that insensitive lab girl's head on a platter. Where was everyone? I was still fuming when the lab girl emerged from Harriett's room, saying, "She'll go up soon." Paul, Hillary, and I rushed back in, and a suddenly mellow Harriett greeted us.

"Wanna know the lab girl's theory of the crime?" Harriett's loopy grin revealed that the hypo had kicked in.

"Yeah," I said dumbly.

"Al Cowan," Harriett whispered.

She spun a story about the driver of the white Bronco pretending to be O. J.'s pal, but really having a thing for Nicole. . . . I gave up trying to follow the complex scenario. Harriett's anxiety was over for today. She chuckled, aware of the irony of slipping into the fantasy world of other people's horrors: Brentwood, the glove, Kato, Mezzaluna. I blessed the lab girl and the TV.

Harriett supervised the head shaving, and we said good-bye as she was wheeled into surgery. The long wait began. Paul got a soda. Hillary called a high school friend. I tried to read. We watched the trial, endlessly. We ate. We talked. Sometime that day, Paul told me, "The last good man I voted for was Barry Goldwater." Recalling Harriett's fervor for the other side back then, I thought about how unimportant politics is to marriage.

Eight hours later Harriett was in recovery. The doctor told us that he'd found a hemangioma, much rarer than the acoustic neuroma he'd expected. Paul asked the exhausted doctor to accompany us to see Harriett, saying, "My wife has spent months becoming an expert on acoustic neuroma. When she hears you found something else, she'll have a million questions. We need you there." How well this man knows my sister, I thought.

Isaiah warns a worldly people about God's anger and consoles them with God's mercy. This intense prophet also has a taste for the ludicrous, as shown in his portrayal of the clay pot that dares to talk back to the Potter. The pot's challenge to her Creator, "What are you doing?" (45:9), is comical because it's so oddly human. When God's face is hidden, we're left to our own devices. Sometimes the Spirit is housed in laughter.

In times of trouble, hope most helpfully coexists with a gritty realism. The Lamb of God is not Mary's cuddly little pet, but

someone we're going to slaughter. Jesus is truly human when he
wails, "My God, why have you forsaken me?" Job is more real
railing against a silent God than after his renewed prosperity.
Later blessings don't mitigate past horrors; new children don't
replace those he lost. Harriett says that even when it's all over,
Job isn't able to laugh at his friends' attempts to comfort—or
confront—him with self-serving pieties. They're comical only to
those of us removed from the suffering; they actually increase
Job's pain.

When Job asks, "Why me?" his friends say, "Because (unlike
us) you have sinned." God's silence says, "Why not you?" Job's
friends' religiosity has strong roots. Their god is the comedian's
thin-lipped Church Lady, saying, "I gave you cancer, or AIDS,
because you are evil." Job's why is never answered, but he meets
God through suffering, when time stands still. Painful, scary
places seem to be God's favorite meeting ground.

When health returns after a serious illness, time continues
to be suspended long enough to usher in awe and humility.
Renewed creation blossoms in awakening to the murmurs of
those you love, the taste of lemon pudding, the clouds floating
past your window, the miracle of taking your first wobbly steps.

The sound of my sister's laughter renewed me, no longer
laughter to ward off our fears, but to share relief and gratitude
for complex skills and simple blessings.

The next morning, I found Harriett sleeping. Intensive
care patients were hooked up to machines and monitored by
nurses who sat at the foot of each bed. Harriett opened her
eyes and beckoned me over. She had a story.

In the middle of the night, Harriett had been awakened
by noise. Assuming the unconscious, hearing-impaired
patients would never know, the ICU nurses had a TV set
tuned to the nighttime replay of the Simpson trial. Harriett

pulled off her oxygen mask and demanded that her nurse turn down the set so she could get some rest. The embarrassed woman apologized, astonished that O. J.'s drama had penetrated anesthetic fog, head bandages, even a hearing impairment. We had our first post-op laugh.

Visiting hours began later in the morning after Harriett was moved out of intensive care, so I asked the hotel's driver if we could swing over to the courthouse. He smiled, saying that eventually most of the patients' relatives made this request. I had heard you could buy buttons with photos of your favorite character from the trial—attorneys or witnesses—from vendors on the courthouse steps. Only in America. I got several buttons.

Outside of the door to Harriett's room, I put on a Judge Lance Ito button, planning to keep it covered until I determined her condition. I opened the door, saw that Paul was with her and that she seemed better. Grateful for my new brother-in-law and for her improvement, I flashed the Lance Ito button. We felt graced.

I pray that Harriett and I retain the ability to laugh at our wonderful, silly world. She has a tumor on the other side of her head too.

Perfection Salad at Iowa's Orange-Spectrum Funeral Buffet

The ubiquitous Jell-O appears at Iowa occasions big and small, as appetizer and/or salad and/or dessert.

SECOND SUNDAY

*[John's] food was locusts and wild honey. At that time
Jerusalem, all Judea, and the whole region around the
Jordan were going out to him.*

—Matthew 3:4–5

My grandson Jacob and I were making an edible brain.
We had a mold shaped like a human brain, only big-
ger. It was meant to be a gag—literally. We relished the
prospect of serving it to Jacob's uncles, boys of forty- and
twenty-something who laugh at whatever disgusts and
delights ten-year-olds. We'd bring the gray matter to the
table, quivering on a platter, take out a sharp knife, and . . .
dissect and serve.

Jacob read the instructions: "After it has jelled, remove
from refrigerator and beat with a mixer, adding one can condensed milk."

I'd surely never made a gelatin brain before, so why did this
seem familiar? "When smooth, place in well-greased mold."

This bizarre concoction was new to me, so why this *déjà
goo*?

When I shook it out onto the platter, I knew. Of course! This edible horror was Momma's masterpiece (without the graham-cracker crust and in a different shape). It was our family's favorite dessert in the fifties.

Momma always said she was no cook, though my sisters and I preferred her cooking to anyone else's. I suspect she didn't like to cook, but back then not cooking wasn't an option for women. She often used recipes from food packages, such as the gelatin dessert that my sisters and I now call "Momma's Pink Cake."

When she cut recipes from the paper, she referred to those dishes by the name of the woman whom the food section had featured. I eventually learned from in-laws that other families' favorite dishes were passed on with a relative's name: "Lee Reinisch's Cheesecake," "Wen Dechant's Christmas Sausage," "Chong Twanmo's Noodle Soup." But we called our favorite dishes by the names of the people who'd given them to the *Des Moines Register,* reflecting, I guess, Momma's lifelong protests that she was no cook, along with her concern that taking credit for those recipes would be a kind of culinary plagiarism. Throughout my childhood, our family birthday celebrations featured "Mrs. Hatch's Chocolate Cake," though we knew Mrs. Hatch solely by that cake.

When packaged mixes came on the market, Momma embraced them, and the faceless Mrs. Hatch and her recipe became nostalgia. Cakes were still frosted with "Modena Jones's Icing," though. We did know Modena, who'd worked for us when Momma was sick. By the time we learned that the frosting's basic ingredient was Crisco, we loved it too much to accept anything else. Modena, who'd worked in a bakery, said it was what the professionals used.

Momma has a lifelong reminder of what she did for love in the kitchen. She got her fingers caught in the electric mixer while making icing for my fifteenth birthday cake. She was rushed to the emergency room, her fingers still entwined in the beaters, bloody Crisco and all. The injury required many stitches and resulted in a numbness that permanently affected her ability to type.

The ubiquitous Jell-O was loved for its versatility. Enhanced with fruit cocktail, shredded vegetables, whipped cream, or cottage cheese, it could be appetizer, salad, or dessert. "Perfection Salad"—a concoction with shredded cabbage, carrots, pimentos, and pickles suspended in gelatin—became the most popular salad of the time when cooking got promoted to "domestic science" or "home economics" and mastering it was central to a woman's worth.

A short-lived "surprise ingredient" fad emerged in the sixties: meatballs that required a jar of grape jelly; cakes made with mayonnaise or soda pop; something called "Mock Apple Pie" made with Ritz crackers instead of apples. Substitutions were celebrated for novelty rather than nutritional merit. We don't eat like that anymore.

Except at funerals. At Grandma Dorothy Dechant Papich's funeral, the ladies of Visitation Church prepared lunch, as they always do. I hadn't been in the church basement since I was in eighth grade, so I noticed the new electronic bingo board right away. Everything else—including the food—was the same, thank goodness. The ladies served what I have come to think of as Iowa's orange-spectrum funeral buffet. Ignoring fussy nutritionists who mandate a color balance, this monochromatic meal was perfect, even on an August afternoon in the still-not-air-conditioned church: baked ham decorated with maraschino cherries and pineapple, au gratin potatoes, sliced tomatoes, orange Jell-O, deviled eggs, and lemonade.

Cholesterol isn't counted at funeral meals, where warm, familiar, hardy food consoles. When death marks the end of an era, you celebrate family and friends and history, along with the life from which it all sprung. All that cooking and caring and eating and sharing nourishes us. We're reminded to celebrate life as we honor death.

Everyone comes out to be with John the Baptist, if not to sit at his table. The recording of his bizarre diet suggests that he invites people to share it; surely he doesn't eat in front of those who have traveled a long distance to see him. Some probably do eat with him, but it is the prophet's consolation and challenge that nourish them: Prepare for wonder, mercy, grace; shed that old skin of envy and pettiness; reinvent yourself as a loving and just person.

God sends the Israelites manna in the desert, and that modest meal becomes salvation. Passover and communion re-create sacred history at the table. Jesus takes pity on the crowds that follow him and feeds them before he preaches. Today some soup kitchens run by religious establishments force the homeless to attend a prayer service before feeding them, a form of extortion contrary to their founder's practice and spirit. Jesus knows that an empty stomach can't host the movement of the Spirit. He eats with all kinds of people, elevating simple meals to celebrations of intimacy and creating bonds of commitment. Fellowship is a part of his sacred message when tables become altars.

It is good to remember that Wisdom offers life-giving nourishment at her banquet (Prov. 9–10) and invites the humble, the just, the kind, and those who seek discipline and understanding. Ancient and modern miracles occur at meals with those who love, even in difficult times. And the only thing I must bring to Wisdom's table is my hunger.

Momma's Pink Cake
serves 8

2 packages JELL-O brand
strawberry flavored gelatin dessert

2 cups hot water
Juice of two lemons

Let gel in icebox til thick (spoon makes an impression in it).
Then beat on high speed. In other bowl beat:

2 cans condensed milk

½ cup sugar

When thick, fold this into gelatin mixture. Cover greased pan
with graham-cracker crumbs. Pour mixture in and spread
more crumbs on top. Refrigerate until serving. (To make
brain mold, omit lemon and sugar. Add green food coloring
to get a gray color. Pour into well-oiled brain mold.)

Modena Jones's Icing
covers a 3-layer cake

1 cup Crisco
½ cup butter
3 tablespoons flour
3 cups powdered sugar

1 egg, optional*
Vanilla
Fruit juice, if desired

Beat butter and Crisco together until fluffy, then add rest.

*Best to omit in these salmonella-plagued times.

Isaiah's Dream

*My great-grandparents Robert Dyer Reed Topliff
and Abigail Hawkins Topliff are the only two who could
have said if their seventy-four-year marriage was happy—
but the evidence indicates they'd disagree.*

SECOND MONDAY

A highway will be there,
called the holy way; ...
It is for those with a journey to make,
and on it the redeemed will walk.

—*Isaiah 35:8–9*

Grandma Miller and her sister Ernestine called their mother "difficult," and worse. Ernestine said that her mother had been "spoiled rotten" as the only girl in a family with seven boys. Grandma blamed her mother's crankiness on a hearing loss that made her think everyone was talking about her. Everyone probably was.

Great-Grandma suffered in comparison to her husband, whom their daughters idolized. He was a homesteader, then a U.S. marshal at the Iowa-Missouri border during Jesse James's days. His daughters saw him as adventuresome and courageous, their mother as a woman who always thwarted his wanderlust.

My sisters and I never had the opportunity to know the other two daughters, but Grandma and Ernestine both claimed to be their father's favorite. "Dad and I got along like two turtlebugs," Ernestine said. "I was his pet, even though I was a brat." Grandma said, "Dad thought the sun rose and set on me." Both were irked at the way their father "waited on Mother hand and foot."

In 1948 Ernestine asked her father, then ninety-nine, to dictate the story of his life. Thirty years later my sisters and I obtained this story, which told of frontier America and gave us a rare insight into—and a new perspective on—his marriage.

The Topliffs had come to the new state of Iowa by covered wagon from Ohio with their ten children. An eleventh child, Robert Dyer Reed Topliff, was born in Iowa in 1849. (Robert would become my great-grandfather, the father who Grandma and her sister adored.)

Robert's mother was "stricken with the quinsy" and died when he was only four. Placed with relatives in Ohio, Robert never saw his father again. His memoir hints at the loneliness of a hardscrabble life: "There were five girls and one boy in the family I went to live with. . . . I remember my aunt said after I had been there a while, 'I guess Robert is not a very bad little boy.' I have never forgotten that—and I think it has had a bearing on my life."

At fifteen, Robert went off on his own to enlist as a soldier in the Civil War but was rejected for being too young. He recounts, "My uncle gave me a colt, and when he died I sold it. . . . Though I claimed it, it really didn't belong to me any more than anything else; I guess I just had to have something to call my own. I took the money, and went back to Iowa, where my relatives were." Before he got there, a catastrophe stunned America: the president had been shot in a theater.

On April 15, 1865, the *New York Herald* reported:

> The screams of Mrs. Lincoln first disclosed the fact to the audience that the President had been shot. . . . Mrs. Lincoln wailed, "Oh, why didn't they shoot me?"

The paper details that an assassin had leapt from the wings, and playgoers

> rushed towards the stage, . . . exclaiming, "Hang him! Hang him!" The excitement was of the wildest possible description. . . . The popular heart is deeply stirred . . . the people, with pale faces and compressed lips, crowded every place where there was the slightest chance of obtaining information. . . . The entire city tonight presents a scene of wild excitement, accompanied by violent expression of indignation and the profoundest sorrow. . . . The [bedside] parting of the President with his family is too sad for description.

Robert's own account tells of mourning alone out on the Great Plains: "Lincoln's assassination left our part of the country dumbfounded. He was brought back to Illinois to be buried, and I drove a one-horse wagon to the railroad intersection, loaded with hickory bark, in order to have a big enough bonfire to see the train go through."

In Iowa, Robert married Abigail Hawkins. "I was nineteen, she was seventeen. All Abigail's family lived in Postville, Iowa . . . and she, being accomplished in an aesthetic manner, drew a great deal of happiness from being among the people she loved—from following the civilized life they had established. . . .

"I was all for striking out on our own and staking a claim. . . . I had pioneer blood in me . . . and didn't mind the hardships, the meager living, and I guess I expected her to think like I did. We went to Minnesota to stake a claim . . . . traveled 200 miles, the last fifty miles we had to take the wheels off the wagon and make it into a sled to get through the snow."

They rented an old shack where Robert broke twenty-five acres. "We lived on fish, geese and swan . . . but my wife got so homesick. . . . I had to take her back to her mother. The rough kind of living was too much for her."

Next spring, Robert struck out again, this time building a house before sending for Abigail. "I put the roof on, then put sod on top of the roof to keep the weather out. . . . But one day, much later, the roof fell in anyhow—while my wife and daughter were outside. They were pretty nearly frightened to death, but unharmed.

"My wife didn't like roughing it any better the second try. . . . We went back to Iowa. I traded my oxen for horses, and I traded my reaper, team, harness, wagon and bobsled away. I didn't calculate I would ever go back. . . . As my wife seemed not to be happy any place else, I set out to make a living [in Postville, Iowa]."

Robert traded all the profits from his land for the rights to sell a newly patented invention. "I found I couldn't make more than a meager living. My wife was making more than I as a milliner and dressmaker. She had an abundance of natural talent; she could do anything she ever saw anyone else do. My nephew killed a swan one day. . . . My wife tanned the hide herself, tore it up in little strips, and trimmed coats for the children. These swansdown coats were in the family for years."

This young man bristled at being surrounded by in-laws who "were well off, and tried to boss [him]." So he struck out again. Months later, Abigail joined him in Missouri, "but she became afraid of the Ku Klux Klan, and begged me to take her . . . north into Iowa. Missouri was too wild for her; she felt she was in wooly territory. So I put everything I had in the wagon and went to the Iowa line. We had six dollars."

Robert worked at many trades for the next twenty-nine years, but he was a farmer at heart. Though she preferred life in town, Abigail settled for a pine house on rented acres, with their own chickens, horses, cows, and gardens.

Missouri didn't have prohibition, as Iowa did, and nearby Davis City, a notoriously rough and tumbling border town, elected Robert marshal before he was thirty. At that time, early arrests usually followed "a fight of the flesh"; Robert didn't carry a gun. He developed a surprise kick to the stomach that knocked the wind out of the lawbreakers. After Robert was shot in the jaw and his deputy killed in the line of duty, the town bought Robert a gun.

One night some outlaws looking for Robert came to his home, where Abigail was alone with the girls. They did no harm, but it isn't difficult to imagine her fear of the escalating violence. Discontent increased when she became pregnant with what they used to call "a change-of-life baby." Ernestine was born when the other girls were eighteen and twenty and Grandma was thirteen. Robert remained marshal for twenty-five years off and on, though the town couldn't afford to pay him regularly.

By the time she and Robert were in their fifties, their oldest three daughters were married, and Ernestine was twelve, Abigail must have thought they were settled into what was then old age.

She was wrong.

Isaiah dreams of springs bursting forth in the desert, yielding abundant flowers and greenery. A highway stretches across this lush landscape; it is the way out of sorrow to new life. The blind see, the deaf hear, the lame leap, and the mute sing as they dance along this road, freed from suffering.

Others look at that desert and see a parched death trap where thieves lurk and beasts wait to devour them.

Centuries later Jesus asks, "Who do you say that I am?" and the beholders reveal themselves: Jesus is a blasphemer, a redeemer, a magician, a miracle worker, a prophet, a con man. His followers are Irish and English, popes and Klansmen. They demonstrate against the death penalty in Texas and burn women to death in Salem. They wear Quaker bonnets and military uniforms. They are slave traders and abolitionists.

I create God in my own image and likeness, too. God and I are so much alike that She demands very little of me.

Christ, Isaiah, and other pioneers hold out a vision: Abandon your idols, honor your covenants, strive for justice. Then take the highway to the Promised Land.

Needless to say, it is always a toll road.

In 1904 Robert "took a notion" to move to California. Ernestine says her mother "hit the ceiling." Again, Robert went on ahead. The West is booming, he wrote. Protesting the whole time, Abigail sold the Iowa house and all their belongings. They used the fifteen hundred dollars to buy land in Pasadena. Later they bought acres in the San Joaquin Valley, then in Burbank and Glendale. Robert made more money in his first nine months in California than he'd made in all his years in Iowa. They had arrived in the Promised Land, and even Abigail thought it was wonderful. They lived off income from property there until they died at ages ninety-two and one hundred.

As an elderly widower, Robert still seemed awed at his good fortune in marrying Abigail: "We were different, we two, there's no denying; she was much smarter than I, had family ties and cultural patterns ingrained that I never knew. She was too smart to lead a pioneer's life. Looking back, she must have thought a good deal of me to have followed me about the way she did."

Abigail died in 1943, a few months short of their seventy-fifth wedding anniversary. Their story suggests that we can never really understand someone else's marriage, even that of our parents. Their daughters' relatively few years at home coincided with difficult times in their parents' marriage; the girls' image of a discontented mother was forever fixed. Their father looked back over a much longer span of wedded life and felt blessed by the refined woman who'd shared it with him. Most of their married years were spent in California, the land perfectly tuned to Robert's talents and temperament and to Abigail's yearning for a place she could call home.

The Cat That Kept Going Home

Stripey examines a Christmas toy in the new house, no doubt awaiting her chance to be let out so she can return to the old place again.

SECOND TUESDAY

In the desert prepare the way of the LORD!
Make straight in the wasteland a highway for our God!
—*Isaiah 40:3*

Stripey kept vanishing after we moved. Our former neighbor Mrs. Billings would call Momma to say, "She's back," often before we even noticed the cat was gone. It was difficult enough for our family to find each other in the new house, amid all those high-ceiling rooms with their massive sliding pocket doors.

How does she find her way back to the old house? the adults kept saying. Yet something in me sympathized with the cat's need to keep padding all the way back, then to yowl when she found strangers in our old bungalow.

There was plenty for a cat—or a child—to explore in the new neighborhood. Ours was one of only three houses high up in the center of Thompson's Bend over the Des Moines River. The O'Dea brothers had lived in the two houses to the north forever. At the south end, a huge gully had housed shacks for ice storage at the turn of the century. Now my sisters and I grabbed tree branches and swung our way down into the woodsy ravine, crunching acorns under our shoes as we ran to the river, an adventure all the more enticing because it was forbidden.

I wandered through our new house, awed by stained-glass windows that ascended the wall by the carved cherry staircase. Forty years earlier, the Gordon girl had been married here; her groom had worn his World War I army uniform. "Can't you just see the bride coming down this stairway?" Momma would say, pointing to the fruit and flowers carved into the woodwork. "They don't make houses like this anymore."

Kathleen and I were happy to continue sharing a bedroom because we were even more afraid of the dark in the new house. Even in our old tiny bungalow, nighttime shrieks from the alley behind our house spooked us, though we knew they were just tomcats. Now, alien nocturnal creatures squeaked and hooted from the gully—could they come in our window? The house itself shuddered at night—were those groaning and creaking sounds monsters creeping up the staircase?

We didn't envy Harriett for getting her own room, even though it was the most beautiful of all the bedrooms and the focus of everyone's efforts.

Looking out her windows at the back of the house, Harriett had a spectacular view (as if a baby could appreciate it) of the river. Windows everywhere—even in her closet—made her room light and airy, along with all those delicious pale colors: wood the shade of clover honey, carpet that Momma called champagne beige. Grandma made drapes of unbleached muslin, like luminous eggshells, to filter the sunlight. Kathleen and I had helped make fringe for the drapes that summer, wrapping string around a *Reader's Digest* sixteen times, then tying it off so Grandma could crochet each tassel into a strip.

Colored tiles in geometric designs were set into the bed's wooden headboard. The bedroom set came from Chicago, where it had belonged to the Armours, who ran a big slaughterhouse, the antique dealer told Momma. Harriett still slept in her crib; she wasn't big enough for the high double bed yet. Such a baby: she whined every morning that butterflies bothered her at night, and Momma had to keep telling her it was only a dream.

Did fear creep into that house right at the beginning? Or did it start when Momma discovered that bats were coming down the bedroom fireplace after dark, flapping into Harriett's crib?

In our old neighborhood, no one locked houses or cars. Even the tramps who carved the phone poles to mark the homes that gave food were not considered dangerous, just hungry. Our new next-door neighbor, Mr. O'Dea, told Daddy he slept with a gun under his pillow, which made us as afraid of him as of the robbers he feared. The older O'Dea brother, his elderly wife, and a caretaker lived in the house to the north of the younger one. Their caregiver told Momma she found a lump in the pocket when she was ironing old Mrs. O'Dea's dress. She was horrified to discover it was a dead canary. Did the old lady kill it or find it dead before stuffing it in her pocket? Within a year, the elder brother climbed the dome of the Iowa state capitol building and jumped to his death. Such terrible things had never happened back on East Twelfth Street. Can a house be a home when you don't feel safe in it?

We were different, too, in the big new house with all the antiques and other finery to protect, isolated, with few neighbors, and Daddy was spending more time at work. Then depression descended upon Momma along with menopause. We girls tiptoed around the house, trying not to disturb her and unearth other troubles. Daddy bought a rifle, the first real gun we'd ever seen, and mounted it over the fireplace. Was he becoming like the O'Dea brothers? Can houses remodel people?

We gave Stripey to Grandma and got a collie to be a watchdog. But the hacking sound of motorboats on the river terrorized Prince. We crawled behind the bushes with his food, coaxing our whimpering protector to eat. Anxiety seemed always in the air then, like the bats circling our chimneys.

The new place makes everything different. It and I and we are different during this time of change. It's frightening to become a lonely exile in what is supposed to be home.

Isaiah holds out hope to a people like this, a people exiled so long in Babylon that their grown children have never known what they all call "home." What is home? All we know is that home is the place of our early dreams about what we'd become and do, in that once-upon-a-time place we like to recall as ideal. Now it is our memory of those early hopes. Remember the time before we knew that real people carried guns and the world could be a strange and dangerous place? Remember God's promise . . . when we were young?

"Make straight in the wasteland a highway" back home to Jerusalem, the Promised Land, Isaiah urges (40:3). Your exile is over. Some are ready to go, but those who have grown old in exile are skeptical (just ask Moses). The grumblers discourage hope; it's easier to prepare for disappointment than it is to expect an encounter with God. What if we return home and find we no longer belong there either? Remember the high cost we paid when our hopes were dashed?

Prophets urge a new hope. Remember the high cost of refusing to hope?

Isaiah's poem also offers a hint of death, the death in every leave-taking, even when we are returning home. "The grass withers, the flower wilts" (40:7); earthly glory is transitory. Believing that security or permanence can be found in places and things is an illusion. The neighborhood has changed, and so have we. Don't you recall burning your mortgage on this old place? Why are you making so much out of a structure? Mature hope relies on higher values.

For a while in alien surroundings the exiles lament, "How could we sing a song of the Lord / in a foreign land?" (Ps. 137:4). I wondered this, too, as a child, displaced. But I did learn to sing a new song in a different place. I became different, too: at first insecure, lonely, stumbling, eventually stronger.

But sometimes—when in turmoil—I yearn to go back to other times and places where I felt safe. I long to stand in yesterday's doorway, to be sheltered from the elements but on the threshold of promise, to believe I will depart only in my own time and for a better place.

Remember . . . when we were blessed? Remember . . . when we couldn't wait to grow up and get going?

Mrs. Billings would make cinnamon rolls to celebrate my coming back to visit. Cloth-covered bowls of dough roosted on the floor, plumped by hot air from the register. From her warm, yeasty-smelling kitchen, I could look out the window to the rock garden where Stripey had kittens. When I left, I'd be on the sidewalk where Daddy taught me to ride a two-wheeled bike, past the corner lot where Sarah Nass told Kathleen and me the truth about Santa Claus. In the new neighborhood, we were the only kids. No one shouted, "Oly, oly, oxen free" or "Trick or treat." No kick-the-can or lemonade stands or red rover.

Within a couple of years, Kathleen and I became teenagers who met our friends on the phone and no longer cared about such childish things. When Mrs. Billings called, I didn't want to go back to the old neighborhood to see an old lady who didn't even have a TV set. The "new" house, where the phone was, had become home, familiar, safe.

The Swansons bought the house from our family in 1962, sixteen years after we'd moved into it, and Mrs. Swanson lives there to this day. She is nice when my sisters and I go back to visit. She also had three daughters and understands our need to say to spouses and children:

"This was my room."

"This was Harriett's fireplace, where the bats came in."

"This is where I'm from."

Like Stripey, I pad back to the old home, the birthplace of so many stories, on foot or in memory. The old neighborhood has changed and so have I. But high up there on Thompson's Bend, it offers a clear vista of where I've been, where I am now, who I'm becoming or failing to become. On a clear day I might even see the place I hope to get to, and a bit of that old fear of change is triggered, along with the hope that if I fall, I'll land on my feet.

If Hope Were a Country

*I thought of hope as virtue gracing an individual.
Then I saw an entire people energized, united, and
led by a hope symbolized by an image of Mary.*

SECOND WEDNESDAY

They that hope in the LORD will renew their strength,
  they will soar as with eagles' wings;
They will run and not grow weary,
  walk and not grow faint.

—Isaiah 40:31

Scott Olson was on the phone, apologizing about such short notice, but could I take an unusual job? In Wroclaw, Poland? And, uh, there's no pay . . . though travel expenses are covered. It was an offer I couldn't refuse. After embracing democracy, Poland wanted information on working with media in a free society. The need was greatest in the Lower Silesian area of Wroclaw, which had less contact with the West than cities like Warsaw.

We were soon on our way to a country liberated after fifty dismal years of Communism, the entire life span of most of its citizens. We found a gray, cold, snowy land and a warm people. Americans were welcomed with invitations to people's homes, offered rides to local sites, bombarded with questions that presumed we knew about every conceivable business enterprise. The gracious, enthusiastic Poles were proud of their grassroots defeat of totalitarianism, grateful the entire free world had cheered them on, exhilarated to face a future in which anything seemed possible. If hope were a country, it would have been Poland in 1992.

I joined Scott, a college professor, to give a communications workshop. He covered theory for the academics in the audience; I represented the working world of public relations for the entrepreneurs and government workers. Many attendees had been in jail or mental hospitals for opposing Communism. Government workers were former activists appointed in the new society to positions in arts, recreation, and tourism as a reward for Solidarity leadership. They were excited about inventing their own jobs providing information to a free people.

I soon learned I needed a crash course in living under a system in which rude and sometimes brutal politicians had communicated to the people through accusations, propaganda, or force. Our cultural differences became apparent when my translator told me there is no word in the Polish language for "communications." A phrase—on the order of "transportation of ideas and images"—was used to convey this new concept. They just said "public relations" in English, like "cowboy," "jeans," and "Coke."

Days were exciting and exhausting. I was often up past midnight redesigning the next day's sessions based on what I'd learned that day. Then, overstimulated, I'd lie awake thinking of different individuals:

❖ Jerzy, who had dreamt of independent radio in a free Poland during his days as chief of Underground Radio Solidarity. Now he was working on a media kit to announce the opening of his station, whose call letters translated to the word "dream."

❖ Jacek, whose entrepreneurial spirit blossomed when he

saw the unbelievable truck lines waiting to cross the borders in and out of Poland. He came to the workshop to design a brochure headlined *Want to Avoid That 24-Hour Wait at the Border?* He left, ready to launch his new air-shipping company.

❖ Eva, an English literature professor, had phony business cards printed to cut red tape and get a phone. It worked: she got the phone. Then it rang. A woman called for help advertising her new business. Embarrassed to admit she wasn't a real business consultant, Eva tried some ideas. They worked, and the client told others. Eva ambushed me after a session, her eyes wide with fear:

"I've been doing 'public relations,' without even knowing what it was called, and I have no qualifications. Now I'm getting requests to help others. What should I do? I know nothing of business."

"You've already solved the toughest business problem, getting customers." I laughed. "Obviously, you're doing something right."

Eventually Eva saw that she didn't have a problem: she had a second career.

The Poles are like the Israelites: a people on the threshold of freedom. Isaiah assures Israel that the Lord of history is at work in political movements. Even the powerless can remind rulers and citizens to seek God's will. They are called to pioneer a new order. Their land is to be the center of the redeemed world, a holy place.

Hope is not a virtue of the young who faint and grow weary or stagger and fall, Isaiah says. "Lift up your eyes on high / and see who has created these"—this majestic solar system (40:26). He who names every star will not forget humanity, his most inspired creation. Look to the stars and recall what is precious: our homeland, justice, faith in God. Then hope in the Lord, and you will soar "with wings like eagles" (40:31, NRSV).

Lech Walesa was no longer young in 1980 when he ignited the shipyard strike that led to Solidarity. By 1987 the first Polish pope in history, an elderly pioneer, visited his homeland, reminding people (as if they needed reminding!), "I am a son of this nation and . . . feel profoundly . . . its desire to live in truth, liberty, justice."

Walesa knew John Paul II's visit was the turning point in Poland's struggle for freedom. In a passage reminiscent of Isaiah, Walesa writes, "I felt like Icarus, except that my wings were attached not with wax, but with steel."

How does a short, stocky laborer and father of eight engender enough hope for oppressed people to topple an empire nonviolently? Walesa attributes it to his faith: "Faith was as natural to me as my mother's milk . . . passed from generation to generation because it . . . preserved our national identity and eased our suffering." The Walesas prayed in fields, stables, and kitchens. It was a hard life without a father—he had died from exhaustion two months after being freed from one of Hitler's concentration camps.

The family's yearly Christmas vigil is Walesa's happiest memory. After the priest blessed their cottage, the children ran out to look at the stars. "To commemorate the star of Bethlehem, we never sat down to eat until the first star had risen in the evening sky," he explains. "Later . . . we went to the pasterka, midnight mass. What a celebration!"

Walesa's mother longed to visit Czestochowa, where the miraculous Black Virgin icon is housed at the Paulist monastery of Jasna Góra. Like all Polish mothers, she told her children the legend: how the original Madonna was painted by Saint Luke on a plank from the stable in Bethlehem; how it came to the Paulists in 1384; how the monastery was the only fortress not to fall into Swedish hands in the war of 1655–57; how the monastery's surrender in 1772 marked the beginning of Poland's long history of being ravaged by foreign armies.

Communist authorities constantly attempted to undermine devotion to the image, which for centuries symbolized the triumph of the Church over the state. They even "arrested" the picture to prevent it from touring to Polish churches. In protest, millions attended Masses said in front of empty picture frames. Walesa infuriated his jailers by refusing to remove his Black Virgin pin. The first act of the striking workers in 1980 was to hang an image of the Black Virgin on the gate of the Gdansk shipyards. Years later, Walesa placed his Nobel Peace Prize medal at the Jasna Góra shrine his mother never saw, thanking God that their oppressors' long struggle against the Virgin and the Church had always been futile.

As Isaiah knew, a powerless man revolting against injustice is God's witness to the world.

In 1989 a legal Solidarity won ninety-nine out of a hundred *Senat* seats. In 1990 Walesa was sworn in as president of Poland. When we arrived two years later, rapid changes were under way. Yet some old systems hadn't been replaced. Several hands shot up when I warned the workshop attendees, "Don't speak 'off the record.' Even reporters who turn off their tape recorders are still working."

"Doesn't the authorization take care of that?" someone asked. Neither Scott nor I understood. I asked for clarification.

"Doesn't the reporter get the authorization before the story runs?" the translator said.

Still puzzled, I asked, "What is this 'authorization'?"

Silence. Suddenly the group erupted in laughter and talked excitedly as they grasped the reason for the confusion: even the American president doesn't authorize stories about himself. We now have a free society too!

Polish media had still been getting stories approved by government officials, I learned. They hadn't yet envisioned a truly free press. As they began to do so, euphoria set in.

Followed by panic. The Poles soon realized that a free press also invites pitfalls. Antoni, who directed a medical-engineering firm now paying off debts to a German partner, had to fire a third of the workers to make the business viable. He now feared that reporters, outraged that a former Solidarity union leader could justify firing workers, would ask, "Are you an agent of the Germans?" We rehearsed well-thought-out responses.

The Poles imagined their bosses trapped by antagonistic broadcasters—interviews they'd arranged, a fear their U.S. counterparts share. So we paired up for simulated live, on-camera interviews. The "journalists" and their "guests" anticipated and dealt with loaded questions.

Rehearsal of such interviews was reassuring. Lezcek, playing the journalist, introduced his guest, then quickly lashed out at him with, "Isn't that a *Russian* name you have?" Attendees laughed, applauding Lezcek for thinking of the nastiest question possible in free Poland at that time.

Americans think of hope—along with almost everything else—as a virtue that graces individual lives. That Christmas season in Poland, an entire people was energized, transformed, united, and led by hope. Polish Communism collapsed from the weight of its own inherent weaknesses, but a palpable movement of the Spirit led the Poles in new directions.

A people who had known no other system after more than fifty years of oppression invented a new possibility. Their vision led them to risk martyrdom in pursuit of a nonviolent overthrow of their abusers. This spirit had taken root and ripened long before my visit; they'd begun "transporting ideas and images" of freedom before they had a word for it. In 1992 I was privileged to see the witty, adaptable, ever-hopeful Poles harvesting the fruits of their long, creative journey to justice.

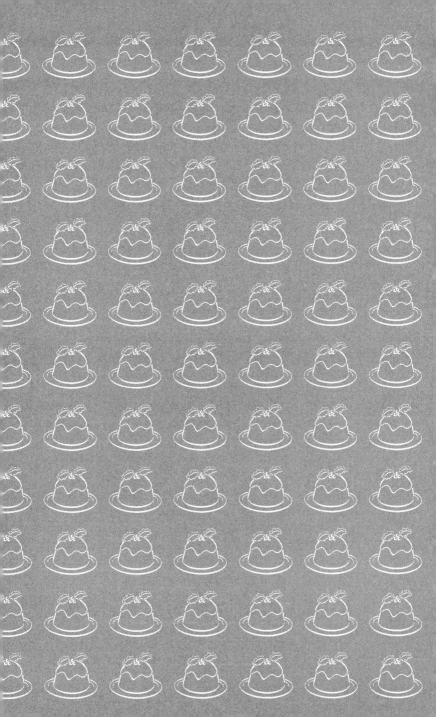

Feeling Tall,
Like the Babe

*During the summer of 1955,
Babe Didrickson Zaharias gave us hope for
ourselves and for our hospital patients.*

SECOND THURSDAY

*I say to you, among those born of women there has
been none greater than John the Baptist.*
                                        —Matthew 11:11

My duties as a nurse's aide included bathing patients,
brushing false teeth, removing catheters and sanitary
napkins, and emptying the patients' ashtrays. Hospital
patients smoked in those days—except those on oxygen—
and most of the doctors did too. I earned sixty cents an hour,
before withholding, that first year when I was sixteen. (The
second summer I gave enemas and got a twenty-cent raise.)

It was a small, thirty-five-bed hospital, almost exclusively
for surgical cases. Most patients had serious conditions; there
was a lot of cancer. News of a cesarean section—much less
common then—created a buzz throughout the hospital, and
all the nurses went to see the infant. New life was celebrated
at Des Moines General Hospital, where it was a rare event.

Four aides rotated among the four floors: Sandra and
Brenda Parsons, Joy Gustavson, and myself. We had to be

there to load and distribute trays for all three meals, then feed patients who needed assistance. So six days a week, we went on duty at 7 A.M. and got off at 7 P.M., spending a three-hour midday break in the nurses' quarters.

Mrs. Potter, our supervisor, was a sturdy, no-nonsense woman, her white RN cap anchored in battleship gray hair. A story circulated that summer that a patient complained to a nurse about the high cost of his hospitalization.

"For this kind money," he moaned, "I could be staying at the Ritz."

"But the bellboys at the Ritz won't give you an enema," the nurse said. It had to be Potter, I thought.

To her, there was a correct way to do everything to benefit the patient and—heaven forbid—an incorrect one: a certain fold and tuck of the washcloth over the hand before bathing the patient; a way of changing sheets with the patient in the bed; proper terms for measuring and charting human waste. Iowa summers before air-conditioning made patients miserable—especially on the fourth floor—so we rubbed their backs with cooling lotion in the heat of the afternoon.

We were not allowed to sit while on duty. If we were without chores for the moment, we walked the halls. Then when a patient rang, we'd get to his bedside faster. Heads and feet of beds had to be cranked by hand, and patients needed to change positions often in the hot, humid weather. No one, not even the RNs, took coffee breaks. We loved it.

Most of all, we adored Potter's can-do attitude. Her son had been a football star at our high school, and she still attended East High games. To her, sports was a metaphor for life: prepare to do your best, go the extra yard, never let your team down.

Potter had the uncanny ability of knowing which patient suffered and which one was a crybaby, and she dispensed sympathy or barked commands accordingly. Once, I tried to ambulate an uncooperative hysterectomy patient who refused to move from her bed. "That woman's a whiner," Potter muttered, marching into the room. She and the patient had already established that their sons had gone to East High. "You need to get up in that chair. Now," Potter said. Two stubborn women took the measure of each other, and Potter and I left the room with the patient in a chair. When I marveled aloud at Potter's easy victory, she scoffed, *"Her* son was just in the band."

Romance even blossomed at the hospital that summer, for one in our ranks at least. The good-looking janitor dated Joy, the petite nurse's aide. The Parsons sisters and I weren't petite. Joy had more fun off duty, but at work Sandra, Brenda, and I had Potter's approval, for we were on the girls' golf team. We didn't tell Potter that athletic ability was not a criterion. Any girl at East who had golf clubs made the team. We placed fourth every season—behind country-club girls in cleated shoes who carried a full set of clubs in leather bags, their woods protected by little booties, and ahead of Tech High, which could never muster an eight-girl team.

That summer the Parsons sisters and I read an article about Babe Didrickson Zaharias in a *Reader's Digest* left in the nurses' station. The story had an inordinate hold on us, not just because Babe was the premier woman golfer of all time, but because we learned that she'd had a colostomy. The writer delicately referred to colostomy as "a difficult operation," but we knew what an understatement that was. Caring for colostomy patients tested our fortitude. We never knew how they coped after they were discharged, but we couldn't imagine they had a decent life with a bag for waste tied to their abdomens.

Babe was also our first ever female hero. She won Olympic gold in track and field, then became a champion golfer. She had a proud husband who encouraged her. She said she won on days when "I feel tall." Three months after her colostomy, she told George Zaharias she felt tall, and she went on to win the U.S. Women's Open by twelve strokes. Babe, who was not petite, gave us hope for ourselves and for those patients whose lives we had feared were joyless. We talked about her all summer.

One day Potter called the Parsons sisters and me to her station. A patient was admitted during the night, she said, a mother of young children. The diagnosis had just come in: polio. Potter said it casually, that word which evoked terror in prevaccine days. Every "polio season," children quit going to swimming pools and playgrounds. Quarantine signs warned people to avoid entire streets where a victim lived. Polio stalked children who enjoyed healthy diets and modern sanitation, as well as children in overcrowded slums.

Since the patient had contaminated the room, the hospital would allow her to stay, the first polio patient for the surgical facility.

"The RNs on the floor have refused to go into the room because they have children at home," Potter said. "I can't ask you girls to do what RNs won't do, so think it over. Let me know tomorrow if you'll work there. If you will, I'll show you the protective procedures."

We were stunned. Potter always expected a lot, but this was a whole new ball game. I felt complimented that Potter handed us this decision. And overwhelmed by it.

"What are you going to do?" I asked Potter, knowing the answer.

"I'll go into the room," she said without blinking. "I believe if you're not afraid of it, you won't get it."

I don't recall if Sandra, Brenda, and I talked about it before going home. I do remember my turmoil that night. If I asked my parents, I could tell Potter they'd said no—an easy out. Yet I'd caught her disappointment in the RNs, and

Potter couldn't administer her floor while providing all the care that this patient required. She needed us as never before. I kept hearing her say, "If you're not afraid of it, you won't get it." But only Potter could not fear polio.

Here comes that twitchy hermit John again. He's a genuine hero for these times according to Jesus, who says to heed careful- ly what John tells me. Okay, there is something compelling about John, but it's certainly not his demeanor—this oddball in a hair shirt who eats bugs! It's that he's calling me to change, to be the best I can be. I'm drawn to this guy's authenticity, but— whew!—sometimes I'd like him to hang in another neighbor- hood, not only because of, let's face it, the way he smells after being in the desert so long. It's that his call sometimes repels me too. My best exceeds my comfort level, and I refuse to budge. Is he asking me to let all those unattractive, starving, lonely, suf- fering, persecuted people pierce the gated community around my heart? Can't all the heroes out there handle it, instead of challenging me? My Inner Hero crouches down, whimpering.

Straight paths offer the toughest walks, and we appreciate heroes only after they're safely dead. John lost his head along with his heart. Jesus was denied and betrayed and crucified. All those prophets and heroes got run out of town and killed. Cancer attacked Babe's spine, this woman with backbone, and she died soon after her comeback. Can John or any of them give me a cost-benefit analysis on rising to difficult occasions? Isn't anyone keeping score?

Sandra, Brenda, and I told Potter we'd do it, and she taught us the procedures. The patient didn't have the bulbar type of polio that would have imprisoned her in an iron lung, and we got to know her well. She talked about her children every day. The work became routine: put a gown over our uniforms when entering the room, remove it before leaving, wear a mask and gloves, wash hands before and after all contact. Nothing else was new.

I didn't think about it during the day. At night, before sleep, I knew I wasn't a real nurse any more than I was a real golfer. I wasn't serving the patients' needs; I was serving my own, wanting Potter to think I wasn't afraid. I prayed not to get caught, to come out of it okay.

I did. The next year Sandra and I graduated, and I went away to college, protected now by the new Salk vaccine. I kept in contact with Sandra for a long time until a Christmas letter was returned "Addressee Unknown."

As a parent, I'm conflicted about what Potter did. How would I feel if she'd given my teenager that choice without consulting me? Yet I'm grateful that I worked under her in my first job.

Sandra: If you read this, let's meet in the twenty-first century at our fiftieth East High reunion. Bring Brenda. We'll compare golf scores without lying, because keeping score was never the point. We'll talk about Babe and about Potter and about how today's teens lack such heroes. We'll give thanks that our children never heard the words "infantile paralysis" and that we came out of that era healthy.

We still won't be petite, Girlfriend, but maybe we'll feel tall.

When Wisdom Spoke and
We Saw Her Beauty

We encountered Wisdom in a Chicago bookstore
one rainy night.

SECOND FRIDAY

Yet time will prove where wisdom lies.
—Matthew 11:19

Esther Williams is five-feet-eight-inches tall; Jackie Onassis wore a nine-and-a-half triple-A shoe; Susan Anton is six-feet-one.

If you remember such statistics but can't quickly recite all of your own phone and fax numbers, I know something about you. You're female and considerably taller than the five-foot-four "average woman." And you shot to your full height and shoe size very young. You'll never forget that year when you suddenly towered over all the kids—and even your teacher.

Different generations of our mothers told tall daughters to take heart, look at Esther or Jackie or Susan. Tall would be okay if gorgeous accompanied it, our daughters reply, but we are not unblemished. Momma speaks of our design flaws as if they stem from blighted branches on the family tree, identifying our guilty Graney, Miller, or Topliff ancestors.

The Graney feet assured that we would surpass Jackie O.'s adult shoe size in fifth grade. By junior high we knew that if the shoe fits, it's ugly.

The Topliff tush is flat and low slung, ever more so with time. Momma tried fanny pads in the fifties but decided the effect was not worth the trouble. To make a good impression, we teach our daughters to confront life—and individuals — head on.

I'm the only one of my generation who inherited the wispy Miller hair. Momma's most frequent hair advice still confuses me: "A short cut is easier. Fortunately, your dad likes short hair on women; most men don't." If Dad didn't like it short, would she adapt to his preference or hold to her own? Do women dress for men or other women or themselves? What does it say about me when I choose one or the other? Perhaps this please-yourself-or-others dilemma is why our family's beauty lore is tongue in chic. It helps keep matters in perspective. Mothers and daughters have to remind each other to draw lines between cost and effect, between being shipshape and going overboard, between what we present and who we really are.

The world is always setting unrealistic and contradictory specifications. Christ's comment in Matthew 11:16–19 shows that even God's chosen ones fail to please others: John is a hermit who fasts, and people call him mad. Jesus eats and drinks with everyone, and people say he's a glutton and a drunkard. They're like children calling to playmates: "We played the flute for you, but you did not dance, we sang a dirge but you did not mourn" (Matt. 11:17).

I'm meant to outgrow these childish entertainments, to abandon callow judgments about others and about myself. Yet I feed on a steady diet of the External Verities: prestige, celebrity, youth, good looks.

Why do we come in so many shapes and sizes, faces, and bodies? What's the point of these variations and our strange judgments of their flaws and merits? When Christ came back to earth in his body, why did all his close friends and followers fail to recognize him? Why did his dear friends know him only after he showed them his wounds?

Once in a while such a rare "Aha!" distracts me from obsession over my own imperfections and longings. An occasional encounter with another's truth—often arrived at through seeing her wounds—provides a glimpse of what will endure. "Time will prove where wisdom lies," Jesus promises, offering hope that humility and compassion may yet triumph over my self-consciousness, this egocentric absorption that obscures valid measures of worth.

"I will be with you always," Jesus says, but perhaps not as I expect to find him. Sometimes Grace appears, as Mother Teresa discovered, in distressing disguises.

It was the kind of group you'd find downtown in Chicago's biggest bookstore in 1980: a hodgepodge of ages and races who'd not otherwise inhabit the same room. They came to hear the author of *How to Write Your Own Life Story* talk about writing memoirs for family history. I was working, so I sat in the back in order to direct latecomers to the speaking area.

Well into the program, the elevator doors opened to reveal a woman unlike anyone I'd ever seen. Her head and face were severely disfigured. She had a disease, I later researched, described by Frederick Treves, a turn-of-the-century physician:

> "[The patient's] most striking feature . . . was his enormous and misshapen head. From the brow there projected a huge bony mass like a loaf, while from the back of the head hung a bag of spongy, fungous-looking skin, the surface of which was

comparable to brown cauliflower . . . [a] growth on the forehead almost occluded one eye. . . . The face was no more capable of expression than a block of gnarled wood. . . . Here was a [person] so vilely deformed that everyone he met confronted him with a look of horror and disgust. Shunned like a leper . . . an object of loathing."

I froze, unsure of how or whether to approach the woman, but she strode purposefully to our group and slid into a chair in the last row. I realized she wished to remain unnoticed, but something unusual struck me when she sat down. In profile, the side of her face near me looked normal. Only her other side was disfigured and misshapen. From my vantage point she looked like an ordinary woman, listening attentively, taking notes.

The author finished her speech and took several questions from the audience. Finally a sixtyish woman in the front row raised her hand. "I know your book isn't about how to get something into print, but I don't have any family to pass my writing to, and I think I have something to say. I'm dying, and I'd like to get an essay published before my time is out. Can you give me any advice?"

The room became still. The author seemed flustered. She said something about finding books on publishing. No one asked more questions; other concerns seemed trivial now. We felt suspended, hoping someone could offer help to grant this final wish.

Mercifully, a voice came from the back row. "I have a suggestion for you." The woman who had hoped to be invisible now stood so the petitioner in front could better see and hear her. Every person stared at the misshapen face, strained to hear the garbled speech. She projected her voice, directing her efforts to the frail lady in front:

"The op-ed section of the Chicago papers sometimes publishes personal essays. I had a piece published a few months ago." She shared how to submit material and advised on length and format.

The dying woman concentrated on their exchange. "What did you write about?"

"Something happened to me. . . . I have neurofibromatosis. The same as Joseph Merrick, 'the Elephant Man.' I seldom go out, but I wanted to see that play. Before the curtain, I overheard a couple behind me talking about what the playbill said about Merrick's history. They'd never heard of this condition. They wondered if it still existed, or ever had.

"I turned around and said, 'I couldn't help but overhear you. I'd be happy to answer your questions about neurofibromatosis, because I have it too.' Just then the lights went out and the curtain rose, so I turned to face the stage, planning to continue the conversation after the first act.

"At intermission, I turned around to speak to the couple, but they were gone. They never returned to their seats. Obviously, my appearance had so frightened them that they snuck out rather than talk to me."

When she was younger, the woman said, she wondered how she would look if she hadn't been born disfigured. So a photographer took a picture of her face, cut the image in half, and flipped the negative so the "normal" side reproduced as its own opposite. She said, "I always imagined that's how I should have looked. But I didn't recognize the girl in the picture. I felt no connection to that image. That's when I began to accept who I am and what I look like."

We strained to hear her voice. "I wanted to tell what my life has taught me: I learned at an early age that people react to the way I look with fear. But what they fear is not me, but something inside themselves. I've learned that those who shun others because we don't measure up to their standards of beauty are far more handicapped than I am."

The silence seemed to offer a holy amen.

"Thank you," the dying woman whispered. Echoing her thanks, the author invited us to a refreshment table. Everyone wanted to connect, to hold on to a moment of grace and truth. We clustered around "the Elephant Woman," eager to speak with her. Across the crowded room, the author and I exchanged a glance. Was this splendid, generous woman an epiphany?

When Dr. Treves discovered his patient Joseph Merrick, he thought—hoped—"the Elephant Man's" spluttering speech and blank look signaled mental retardation. Full awareness of his situation would be too much for any human to bear, the physician thought. Later, after he came to know his patient well, Treves considered the effects of a brutal life upon a sensitive man and judged Merrick to be heroic. Yet the doctor couldn't answer his own question: "How could a person suffer such deprivation of all the sources of happiness, yet remain compassionate and generous?"

In that bookstore on a rainy Chicago night, we asked the same question and had no answer either. We could only be thankful that Wisdom had spoken in that time, in the place where we were, and that we had seen her beauty.

The Unpleasant Exchange at the Shiloh Shoot-Out

After Fred Hahn came through for me, we never again spoke of the Shiloh shoot-out.

SECOND SATURDAY

❧❦❧

Till like a fire there appeared the prophet
whose words were as a flaming furnace . . .
in his zeal he reduced them to straits.
—Sirach 48:1–2

"Think of someone you hate," our writing teacher said. "Describe that person. How does he look? What is she saying?"

Protests erupted. "I don't *hate* anyone," people claimed, struggling with the assignment of portraying villains.

I had no such problem. "Hate" had elicited the powerful image of Jesse J. Elsworth, shoving his chair back to leap to his feet, his face red but otherwise indistinct so many years later. Except for those eyes bulging with fury, lips sputtering venom and self-righteousness. At me.

Dick, a vice president, and I had traveled as a team to bid on what could be a stellar account for the ad agency we represented. We were competing against two other agencies; in corporate terms, we were headed for a shoot-out over the Shiloh Company account. The victor would be awarded a gigantic marketing budget to launch a new product aimed at a Christian market. Our agency had never pitched a contract that big, and I, a nervous neophyte, had worked there less than a month. I'd had little contact with Fred Hahn, our German-born president, until he told me the entire staff planned to celebrate our victorious return.

I was soon standing beside a flip chart addressing Jesse, the elderly philanthropist personally funding the product launch, and four of Shiloh's vice presidents. The excitement level was high because projected sales for the product and its spin-offs were in the millions.

My opening remarks had gone smoothly, and I'd moved into the marketing history of similar products.

Abruptly, Jesse cut in. "May I ask what qualifies you to speak to this group?" His eyes narrowed on me; his tone was angry.

Later I learned that my linking the word "scholarly" with the product's history had triggered his fury. Jesse's upbringing, I found, was contemptuous of egghead Christians, fearing they're on the slippery slope towards nonbelief. At the time, I only knew he wasn't requesting my professional qualifications.

"Are you asking about my religious tradition?" I asked.

"I am asking what Bible you were raised with," he said through clenched teeth.

"The Catholic one. The Douay Version."

Jesse pushed his chair away from the table and glared at Shiloh's executives. "How dare you invite someone to address us who was not raised to love the Word!"

Stunned, I drew in my breath and held it. The Shiloh team had also frozen in place. Dick leapt to his feet to halt Jesse's march to the door.

"Sir, you don't know us," Dick said (meaning *"I'm* not Catholic").

"Right! And I don't *want* to know you people." Rigid with fury, he turned to the Shiloh executives, pointedly giving Dick and me his back. "I'll have no part of them." The door slammed behind him.

Stuck on stage with a pointer in hand, I had no idea what to do next. The executives avoided eye contact with me. Finally, the firm's marketing director—the only other woman in the room—spoke, her eyes downcast. "Carol, on behalf of the Shiloh Company, I offer you our deepest apologies."

I pretended to be magnanimous. "Not at all. Mr. Elsworth had every right to ask that question. And I couldn't lie about my tradition." Seeking a shred of dignity, I said, "Nor will I apologize for it."

The tension eased. The executives asked us to stay. The first round of competition had been a blind shoot-out; the agencies had known little about the product. Shiloh offered us a detailed briefing and several thousand dollars to return for the final competition. Dick seemed relieved. I felt we'd fallen into a bizarre pretend world, where denial of the full implications of their patron Jesse's outburst seemed to extend their apology. Still shocked and embarrassed, I wanted to get out, to fully exhale.

On the plane back to Chicago, Dick and I discussed what we'd learned at the briefing: everyone involved in the project would be expected to sign a "loyalty oath" statement of religious belief, which I couldn't have done. Hoping to be relieved of responsibility for loss of this contract, I wondered if Fred, our agency president, would sign it.

"What religion is Fred?" I asked, praying that "German" meant "Catholic."

"Fred? He's Jewish."

"Would he sign their loyalty statement?"

"They're not concerned with Fred like they are with Catholics." Dick finished his martini and signaled for another.

"They consider him 'incomplete,' still hope to convert him," Dick cackled.

I obviously had a lot to learn. Oddly, Dick still seemed hopeful. It had to be the martinis.

In bed at home that night, replaying the scene, I found my anger for the first time. I represented the ad agency now, which left me no freedom to reject clients, even to acknowledge my outrage at Jesse's insults. By the time the sky turned gray again, I'd vowed to return to freelancing.

The next morning at work, I crept into my office and shut the door. Eventually Fred knocked, then peeked in. I motioned him in. He stood in front of me, bent forward slightly, fingers steepled in an oddly formal gesture. His voice was hushed, as if broadcasting a royal funeral from inside a cathedral.

"Richard has told me what transpired yesterday. And I have told Richard that even if the Shiloh Company executives crawl to Chicago—on their knees—to beg us to participate in another presentation for their contract, we will not do it. This agency will do no further work for the Shiloh Company."

He turned on his heel and left before I could clamp my jaw shut. Fred had made me feel he'd had no regrets about losing his agency's biggest account ever. I laughed, exhilarated, relieved, amazed, feeling immediate kinship with this man I barely knew. He's been my friend for twenty years now. We have never again referred to the unpleasant exchange at the Shiloh shoot-out.

Elijah is the cranky prophet associated with fire; his mouth burns like "a flaming furnace." He is a zealot who reduces people to quivering distress. He ascends to heaven in a fiery chariot. You know the type: subtlety is not in his repertoire.

When Jesus asks, "Who do the crowds say that I am?" some people reply, "Elijah" (Luke 9:18–19), but Jesus links Elijah with John the Baptist (Matt. 11:14), the one who announces the Messiah. In Jewish tradition, Elijah performs wonders in life, and "after death, marvelous deeds" (Sir. 48:14). A master of disguise, he appears as the courtesan who saves Rabbi Nahum's life; as the dentist who cures Rabbi Yehuda ha-Nassi's toothache; and as the kind stranger—the righteous Gentile, the bearer of comfort and hope. He safeguards Jewish communities and visits every Jewish home during the Passover Seder.

The bombastic Elijah has to quiet himself to hear the still, small voice of God, to become a gentler Elijah, though always a man of strong likes and dislikes who speaks the truth.

This prophet's most charming reincarnation is as the jester, the one who makes people stop quarreling and start to laugh. He is the gallant Fred Hahn, making me laugh at my humiliation. Looking back to the events following the Shiloh shoot-out, I see several Elijahs drawing a smile and bringing me peace offerings, even one in the persona of the terrible Jesse J. Elsworth of the Shiloh shoot-out.

I returned to self-employment in fifteen months; Jesse died within a few years. Six years after the shoot-out, an Elijah called, pulling me back to the memory of that difficult episode. This man had recommended me to Shiloh's biggest competitor, whose new product would challenge the one Jesse found me unsuited to launch. Three women executives at the competing company had spent years developing and producing a superior version that was bound to overtake Shiloh's. They hired me to speed up the inevitable victory.

This company found scholarship essential. The principal academic—a man from Jesse's denomination—became my valued colleague. Scores of affiliated scholars from other denominations were instrumental to the historic record the product made and still enjoys. I collaborated happily with them for eight years.

I quit picturing Jesse in Dante's lowest circle of hell and began imagining him alive, fuming at each new sales plateau set by his competitor. I am a deeply flawed person. Then Jim, a man affiliated with the project, mentioned that Jesse Elsworth had been his mentor. "He was one of the most Christian men I've ever known," Jim said. Amazed, I didn't inquire further.

It began to occur to me, though, that while Jesse's behavior was inexcusable, his harsh words were true. Catholics weren't raised "to love the Word" by his standards—those of a man who read the Bible cover to cover every year. Scripture was neglected during my Catholic schooling, an omission being remedied today.

Jesse's upbringing had handicapped him also, with bigotry. Yet Jim had looked at this imperfect man and seen the face of God. I e-mailed him to tell me more.

He replied, "Jesse was the first Christian I met whose management abilities and accomplishments I admired . . . the model I'd been looking for. He was sharp, opinionated, outspoken, very intimidating. . . . I had great respect for him. Hopefully I adopted the good I observed and ignored the rest."

Jim detailed Jesse's generosity, not only of vast sums of money donated to worthy organizations, but also of lifelong, committed volunteerism. He had taught Sunday school for over thirty years.

"It's been inspiring for me to think about him again," Jim wrote. "When he was dying, I visited him. . . . His relationship with his children was not wonderful. Though . . . it is scriptural to 'speak the truth in love,' it [isn't] always well received. Jesse spoke the truth as he saw it. . . . So there was no one else [there] to see him. He had the Bible open on his table. . . .

"He could barely speak. I held his hand, this crusty, old, dying man, and told him I loved him. . . . Two days later he was gone."

Anger is seldom my friend; I can be retaliatory, self-righteous, obsessed with having the last word. But the anger Jesse fueled enabled me to risk self-employment again, to show myself worthy of participating on a project like the one he barred me from, to enjoy the friendship of, learn from, and brainstorm with talented people.

Elijah's successor, Elisha, pleaded for twice his mentor's spiritual powers. Have Jesse's been doubled in Jim? I don't know.

Fifteen years after the shoot-out, I returned to Shiloh. They had asked me to provide staff training, partly because they knew of my success with their competition. Downsizing and attrition assured that I wouldn't run into anyone from that former visit. Showing me around their expanded facility, the sales manager asked, "Have you ever been to Shiloh before?"

"I came to discuss a project once," I replied, imagining the jester-Elijah—with Jesse's face—here with me again, our old quarrel finally dissolving into laughter. "It was a long time ago. Seems like everything here has changed since then."

The Patron Saint of Yentas

*I discovered that the women's side of Israel's
Western Wall "works" equally well.*

THIRD SUNDAY

In everything, by prayer and petition, with thanksgiving, make your requests known to God. Then the peace of God that surpasses all understanding will guard your hearts and minds in Christ Jesus.

—Philippians 4:6–7

A person's prayer is uniquely her own. My friend Renee, a Buddhist, recites a mantra at her computer every morning before working on her novel; other friends meet for small healing services in their homes. One woman went to a river to conduct a private creation ritual, setting afloat items from her past in hope of a better future. Some Chicago cabdrivers travel with prayer rugs, stopping for lunch and worship at a restaurant with a Muslim temple upstairs.

Prayer doesn't need language. My sister-in-law Marianne spends days preparing foods for Passover dinner. In her final weeks with cancer, Cousin Mary Jeanne Powell offered her suffering to God. Grandpa Miller delivered his homegrown corn and tomatoes to our door. Liz Lerman, who directs a national dance company, envisions a time long ago when people danced and their children were healed and crops grew.

Her troupe goes into diverse neighborhoods to choreograph performances with ordinary citizens who have never danced before; elderly, overweight, and wheelchair-bound people learn to create a work of art, body, spirit, and community. Dance can bring peace to the world, Liz believes. Until then, her prayer transforms participants and audiences.

Catholics have traditionally asked saints to intercede on their behalf. When I was a teenager, the most popular saint was Jude, patron of impossible causes (every adolescent's self-image). In my child-rearing days, many expectant mothers decided to name their sons after Saint Gerard, overlooking the gender appropriateness of a male patron of pregnant women. Nor did anyone question how his history applied: Gerard was originally denied acceptance into a religious order because he was simpleminded and tubercular.

Saint Joseph became the unofficial patron of real estate, and his popularity soared during the market crash of the late eighties. Now over two million plastic Saint Joseph statues are sold yearly to Americans who bury him in the yard of the home they want to sell. Enterprising real estate agents have been known to lurk in church-supply stores, burying their business cards in boxes containing his statue. A friend swears there's a saint who will get you a boyfriend, but not, as far as she knows, a patron for breaking up with him.

After favorites like Saint Christopher and Saint Valentine were downsized from sainthood (officially stamped "serious historical problems," Vaticanspeak for "probably a myth"), some Catholics began devotions to the dead-but-not-canonized, such as Padre Pio and Mother Teresa. Some even invoke the help of deceased social activist (and not canonized) Dorothy Day, a woman who feared that sainthood would allow her radical agenda to be too easily dismissed. Such postmodern laypersons envision saying "I told you so" when their role models are officially canonized, whether they're alive to see it or not.

Italians in Chicago's Bridgeport neighborhood have an annual brass-band parade to honor Saint Rocco, a multifaceted holy man. Rocco (aka Rocque and Rock) is invoked on behalf of cattle, doctors, dog lovers, prisoners, and against cholera, skin diseases, and plagues. Bridgeport dogs sport Saint Rocco medals on their collars, commemorating their canine ancestor that licked Rocco's sores and brought him food until he recovered from the black plague. There are patron saints for skaters (Lidwina), cable-TV installers (Gabriel), hairdressers (Martin de Porres), thieves (Dismas), and even lawyers (Thomas More)—so why not for man's best friend?

Are prayers for a New Year's Eve date or a pay raise too trivial and self-centered to bother the Almighty about? Can prayers for victory (on the football field or the battlefield) be justified?

Paul seems to approve of all prayer-filled moments. His epistle from prison exhorts his friends to present every need to heaven in petitions full of gratitude. Thankfulness lays the groundwork for the transformation sought in prayer. Stay faithful to our shared vision of what is good and true, Paul urges. Such a vision leads prophets, artists, heroes, and saints to a numinous life and work. Their light shines, awakening in others a longing to share a higher intelligibility, to transcend ordinary lives with new ways of seeing and being.

Paul endorses every form of prayer, presumably words, motion, work, rest, song and silence, need, anguish, and even confusion and outrage. Can anger at God be "prayer"? The Bible abounds with examples of "Where are You?" echoed in anguish by the psalmist, Job, Jesus, and others. A desperate cry, uttered from a heartsick, outraged, or pain-filled soul suffering shame, injustice, or abandonment, is the most human of prayers.

Perhaps one should mature into praying unselfishly for matters of global importance, but individual petitions for such

mundane matters as getting a job or passing an exam are touch-
ingly heart-of-the-matter. "Give us this day our daily bread"
may have to be put on the altar before "Let there be peace on
earth." Peace must invade human hearts before it can conquer
families, communities, and civilizations.

Some say that the Source of Life doesn't need praise or thanks,
that only humans benefit from a soul-sensibility. But can
Divinity be immanent without a reciprocal relationship with
humankind? Perhaps the Creator needs to be pulled to me, longs
for me to free my mind of myself, waits for me to open my heart
to cultivate memory, hope, and reverence.

Make of this what you will:

We were in Jerusalem at Christmas/Hanukkah time. Our guide, Yussi, a patriot and a poet, was driving us to the Western Wall, the holy site in Israel that once supported the temple. Visitors traditionally tuck prayers into cracks in the Wall, prompting my husband and me to think about a prayer for our six grown children. We decided on this: "That our children will find worthy spouses, if and when they desire to." Yussi chuckled, dismissing this as magical think- ing. American tourists at the Wall amuse him by often asking, "Is it okay to write my prayer in English?" and "Does the women's side of the Wall 'work' as well?" We laughed with him but took our prayers to the Wall anyway. At the time, none of our grown children seemed to have serious marriage prospects, but two, we felt, were ready for them to appear.

Shortly after our return, our daughter Meredith called. We compared New Year's resolutions as we always do. She had been seeing David for years, but she'd bridled at the idea of marriage so often that a long time ago he'd vowed never to bring it up again. That day she'd found the phrase "get married" (in David's handwriting) squeezed into her list of resolutions. Because she laughed when she said it, I suspected this marriage would now happen.

In that conversation, she told me her brother Brian was in love. Within the hour, Linda and Al called to announce their engagement. These weddings (and now a fourth) have all occurred.

The morning after these phone calls, we faxed Yussi in Israel, telling him of the dramatic "results" for three of our children, just two weeks after our visit to the Wall. I added a PS:

"Please tell your American clients that English works fine at the Western Wall and that God does answer the prayers of a woman. (But then, why wouldn't She?)"

(FYI: Every day except Shabbat—sundown Friday to sundown Saturday—faxed prayers are collected and inserted into the Wall. There is no charge for this service, except, of course, the phone-line cost for sending the fax. The number for the Western Wall Prayer Fax Line is 011-972-2561-2222.)

Training Wheels

*Among many other things, Daddy taught me when
to let go of my training wheels.*

THIRD MONDAY

The chief priests and the elders of the people approached
[Jesus] as he was teaching and said, "By what authority are
you doing these things? And who gave you this authority?"
—*Matthew 21:23*

Daddy, at eighty-seven, teaches the art of listening, a daunting task in these times. Long retired as a surgeon, he sometimes lectures today's medical students on diagnosing ailments. He began teaching at what is now the University of Osteopathic Medicine and Health Sciences in Des Moines over fifty years ago. He became a surgeon in the days when there were no antibiotics, nor IVs to hydrate patients during an operation, when large incisions increased the possibility of shock and the only anesthetic was ether, making speedy surgery essential. "We had to get in and out fast," Daddy says.

Now his students enjoy vastly improved conditions, along with state-of-the-art diagnostic equipment such as CT scans, MRIs, and scopes of all types. But for my father, the physician's most important diagnostic tool has always been available: it's the human ear.

The art of taking a patient's history involves skills that can be learned and improved upon, he says, but most of all it involves attentive listening. "If you'll take time to get a good history, and then repeat your history taking from time to time, the patient will give you the diagnosis."

Listening to a tape of my father's lecture to the students, I was reminded of the phone calls from patients that often interrupted our family dinners. Two chronic callers revealed considerable anxiety in their voices and by the length and frequency of their calls. My sisters and I never met Mrs. Brown or Mrs. Hogan, but we knew them by their shaky voices asking to speak to Daddy and by the poinsettia and the *Better Homes and Gardens* subscription they sent our family every Christmas. In my mind I see Daddy, sitting on the sofa in his study, holding the phone to his ear but seldom speaking during these long phone calls. Listening.

I didn't realize then that listening to those fearful complaints had anything to do with healing. I assumed that such calls were an occupational hazard for a man too good-natured to discourage the interruptions of his life. I hadn't learned how a physician's attentiveness validates, consoles, and creates peace as part of his care.

Dad urges students to "spend time with the patient, practice the laying on of hands." I recall an elderly hospital patient when I was a high school nurse's aide. As I was bathing her, she talked about Daddy's hands. "Praise Jesus. He guides that man's hands, yes he does," she said. I knew she wasn't talking about his dexterity as a surgeon but about hands-on caring. I could imagine him holding her hand in the recovery room as she came to, telling her the operation had gone well. Or perhaps he'd placed a hand on her shoulder when he told her she needed the surgery. Still, her fervor seemed strange. I thought she went to Mr. Bogey's church; Catholics, or Presbyterians for that matter, didn't call Jesus by his first name, as if he were a personal friend, right here—dwelling in someone's hands!

I knew Daddy's hands. When he first came home from work, they still had that silvery metallic hospital smell. They steered the car and mowed and raked and guided wood through his electric saw. His right hand waved funny little circles over the paper before setting the pen down to write. Because those hands had once worked at a dry-cleaning shop and were the best at ironing and sewing in our house, they laid a clean sheet over the carpet and pressed Kathleen's wedding gown. They helped me build a pinhole camera for the science fair. I'd looked at his hands all my life, so this woman speaking of his touch as a spiritual experience embarrassed me. I didn't then understand the yearning for human contact when one hears life-changing news, the solace of a reassuring touch.

Keep learning, Daddy says on the tape, for patients can be great teachers to physicians who listen: "Practice the art of history taking, study it, constantly add to your skills." The dedication of the older generation of doctors inspired my father when he was a young man. He admired "their quest to improve and treat, their almost religious devotion to the profession." He promises today's students that health careers will yield a lifetime "of enjoyment and fond memories if you continue to be a student of medicine."

I can't help but wonder, do these medical students understand the authority in his experience, or do they see Daddy as an interesting relic of the era when babies were delivered for ten dollars—as a house call?

Other authorities command their attention during their training experience: drug manufacturers citing cost-benefit ratios of today's powerful medicines (underplaying the importance of taking a careful patient history to detect possibly fatal allergic reactions to such prescriptions); technicians arguing to replace doctors in the diagnostic process with computers; insurance agents urging doctors to see patients as lawsuits waiting to happen; cost-conscious HMO administrators pressuring them to process patients in under fifteen minutes.

Health care ain't simple in this brave new litigious, managed-care world. Will these students remember the simple healing virtues of touching and listening? On whose authority will they rely?

On whose authority do I rely? Do I remember?

"By what authority are you healing people?" the chief priests demand of Jesus (see Matt. 21:23). It isn't a question of what works, but of who has the designated power. Officialdom relies on haves and have-nots: I am empowered; you are not. But when the spiritual becomes elitist (I am sacred; you are profane), it ceases to be holy. When "my church," "my dogma," or "my reading of Scripture" is the Only True Version, divisiveness, not healing, occurs.

Jesus tears down the temple curtain, the one separating the worshipers from the providers, the sacred from the profane. When you're learning, choose your authorities carefully, Jesus says. Avoid false teachers. Don't be awed by power, money, prestige, or today's theories; they won't last. The love of God in your heart is all the authority you need. Then others can no longer tell you who you are, what you can be or do. You will listen to your inner voice, value your own experience, allow ultimate authority to reside within you.

My inner voice is often whiny, often lazy, and much of my experience embarrassing. I'm vulnerable to intelligent persuasion that subtly appeals to the meanness in me. I happily lend authority to witty, urbane voices that identify "the other" as ill-intentioned, unsophisticated, dangerous . . . my enemy. Discernment involves so many pit stops on the journey to truth that my soul frequently hitches a ride with anyone who makes me

laugh at the quest. If only God would give me a clear sign, says
Woody Allen, like making a deposit in my name in a Swiss bank.

Is there a parallel universe, eternity, an afterlife? Should I
give authority to Abraham and the patriarchs, to the healing mir-
acles of Jesus, or to those who dismiss it all? Does Christ heal by lis-
tening and touch, like Daddy? Or is it hypnosis? Or hysteria? Does
faith in Jesus' divine authority act as a placebo?

My soul's journey is still being made with training wheels.
My student days haven't ended, nor has my responsibility to lis-
ten: to hear authentic voices from the past and even ineloquent,
inconvenient, and frequently annoying ones from the present
that might push me along in the right direction.

Fathers and other mentors are training wheels, support-
ing, steering, encouraging you to go out on your own.
Among many other things, Daddy taught me to ride a bike.

A timid, awkward kid with a gory imagination, I envision
broken legs entwined in metal spokes, blood, the neighbors
coming out to stare, sirens, hypodermic needles. I need him
here, holding me up.

I'm off to a wobbly start. "That's it," he says. "You're
doing fine." Fear fades. I'm okay because he's here to keep
me from falling. The wind blows through my hair as we go
faster. This is fun.

Suddenly I notice his hands are gone, no longer on the
handlebar or the seat. He's let go.

I can do it! My own feet propel me now. Exhilarated, I
pedal to Sarah Nass's house at the corner, then skip my foot
along the ground to stop. I turn around eagerly to see him
standing on the sidewalk to show me the spot where he'd
let go. He's way back by the house where the old lady and
her chow dogs with the purple tongues live. He enjoys my
thrill at seeing how far I went on my own, what I did with
his support and his guidance and a little push when he knew

it was time. It's his victory too. I hope the neighbors—the Petersons, the Norpels, the Billings—saw this: me riding a Schwinn without training wheels and Daddy standing there with his hands in his pockets, grinning.

Words: Whispered, Screamed, Stumbled Over, Withheld

*Words matter, but they don't always come easy
to Midwesterners.*

THIRD TUESDAY

A man had two sons. He came to the first and said, "Son, go out and work in the vineyard today." He said in reply, "I will not," but afterwards he changed his mind and went. The man came to the other son and gave the same order. He said in reply, "Yes, sir," but did not go. Which of the two did his father's will?

—Matthew 21:28–31

My friend said, "I love you."

We're fond of each other, of course. But it was a jolt. I wanted to talk to her before I left town. She couldn't clear her schedule, but sensing my agitation, she asked if I was okay. It wasn't life-or-death, I told her. I'd just longed for a girlfriend as a sounding board. She said, "I love you," as if it would have to do.

It did. Those words, so out of the blue and unlike us, blazed in my mind, warmed me. Shortly afterward, I was on the phone with my friend Steve. He'd seemed weak lately, and I asked if he was under the weather.

"It's time to tell you." His voice was hoarse, shaky. "I'm HIV positive."

I was dumbfounded. Steve and his wife, Lois, were dear friends; he was my colleague, a grandfather. I wanted him to take back those terrible words, even as I realized how ill he sounded.

"I'm in my office now. I can tell you're really ill now, so I'll let you go," I said. "I'll call Lois tonight to see how I can help." And then those words leapt out. "I love you."

When I called that night, Lois's first words were, "Secrecy is so awful." Not AIDS. Secrecy. They'd withheld their sad news for nine years, afraid to tell even their dearest friends.

That meant Steve had been HIV positive the entire time I'd known him, when I began volunteering at the social-services agency he ran. I remembered running into him as I was leaving a restaurant one evening years ago. I asked what he was doing there alone. He replied, "Waiting for some friends. I have dinner here every Tuesday with an HIV-positive group." I praised him for his ministry to these others, never suspecting he was trying to tell me he was one of them. I thought of other clues he'd given me over the years, all missed because, surely, AIDS doesn't strike grandfathers.

At his funeral, I thought of Steve's work at a homeless shelter. He never seemed to mind that giving our city's outcasts a meal and kind words was, at best, a Band-Aid for the wounds we allow humans to suffer. Before I knew he was dying, I asked Steve how he kept his humor and, above all, his hope at such a job. "I guess it's just knowing that if I were to quit, I'd be letting down so many friends," he said. I saw now that in his last years he'd directed his depleting energies to what he considered essential.

He couldn't be spared an agonizing death. All I was ever able to do was tell Steve that day, without embarrassment or hesitation, that I loved him. Lois later told me that when he hung up the phone after our conversation, he was so relieved I expressed my love that he lowered his head into his arms and cried.

As their father, I may not see my two sons as clearly as others, but I'll tell you what I see, for what it's worth.

When Matthew writes about them, he seems to be comparing the harlots and tax collectors who eventually follow Christ to those righteous-talking Pharisees who reject him. I hope Matthew is aware of the irony of delivering the message "Actions speak louder than words" in words. I like to think he has a sense of humor as well as a point to make.

John, now, he would have seen us differently if he'd seen fit to tell our story in his Gospel. He knows about the power of words. Like the ancients, John calls God "Word." Word is a verb; it refers to God-filled actions and events throughout history. To announce it, to name it, is to bring it into being. Words have a soul. But it seems that words and actions have become two separate things today, like grammar and poetry.

Would you like my take on my boys' doing or saying (or not doing or saying)? I see it as disposition more'n anything. The older one, he says, "Yes, Papa, sure thing," but he doesn't get around to it. This kid always has a joke for me, though, a smile, a hug. Seems happy just to be with me. He means to do it, see? Sometime.

When I ask the younger boy—the "doer"—he grumbles. Threatens not to do it. Lets me know I'm imposing. Even blames me for making him feel guilty enough to do what I asked. (He feels guilty because he is guilty, but I keep that observation to myself.) Doing counts, but not always more than saying. Words count too.

The way I see it, my boys might still mature into giving me service with a smile. Meanwhile, I'll go on loving the both of them. With fathering, don't you know, it's never just one or t'other.

Words matter. Whispered. Screamed. Stumbled over. Withheld.

I wasn't raised to speak of love. We Iowans of Irish-English-German ancestry tend to be suspicious of effortless affection. As if what comes too easy can't be genuine.

That changed a bit in the sixties, even in the Midwest, when we noticed Johnny Carson begin kissing his female guests hello. We trusted Johnny, a former Iowan, who kissed people stiffly. We noted that only Johnny's substitute male hosts—Californians, i.e., performers—hugged and kissed other males. We tried to become more expressive in those days, but it was easier when other people initiated hugs: McGovern Democrats who invited you over to play Group Therapy, whose peck on the cheek let you know that even though they were over thirty, they still challenged their parents' beliefs. In our family it seemed natural to be openly loving only with the children. My grown children are apt to say "I love you" first, even today.

I had those healing words ready that day for Steve only because someone had just said them to me. We were all blessed.

Upstairs and Downstairs, When We Were Gods

Kathleen (left) and me in 1944, when we were gods,
with Deetoteet, Marjorie, and Zeal standing behind us.

Third Wednesday

The creator of the heavens,
*   who is God,*
The designer and maker of the earth
*   who established it,*
Not creating it to be a waste,
*   but designing it to be lived in.*

—Isaiah 45:18

Fifty years after the time when Kathleen and I were gods we had a Miller cousins reunion. Cousin Janice asked, "Remember Deetoteet, Marjorie, and Zeal?" Of course we recalled our imaginary playmates, but how odd that our older cousin (and her sister Geraldine too, we learned) should remember those bizarre names a half century later. Janice had been away at college then; Geraldine, in high school.

We don't know where the strange names came from, why we created our imaginary playmates, or even how long they were "there," down in our basement playroom on East Twelfth Street. Upstairs, the old bungalow was crowded, especially the tiny bedroom Kathleen and I shared with Harriett and her crib. In the playroom, we lined up our dolls on a big old couch, sat at a table, rolled lumps of clay into a string, and sliced it into "green beans" for a pretend dinner.

Did one fantasy playmate come to us first, I wonder, to be morphed into a trio? And when and how did the adults upstairs become aware of them?

"How is Deetoteet?" Grandma Miller asked one day when we went to her house. "And how is Marjorie?" We reported their well-being and activities. I said they baby-sat for our dolls. I recall Grandma's delight when I told her they'd been naughty and described the punishment I'd given one or more of them. Then Aunt Hilda, who lived down the street from Grandma, also began asking about Deetoteet & Co.

Kathleen and I can't recall how it ended, but our cousins do. One day when Grandma asked about them, Kathleen or I said, "They're dead." The adults were disappointed, aghast; Kathleen and I were unemotional, adamant. Death wasn't negotiable, even in our fantasy kingdom. Janice remembers getting a letter from Aunt Hilda that told of the shocking, intractable demise of Deetoteet, Marjorie, and Zeal.

I don't think it was premeditated murder. Kathleen and I never thought about what we were going to say about the three before we were asked. Perhaps we grew weary of the adults trying to lift the pretend playmates out of our basement sanctuary and bring them up where it was so brightly lit with questions and examination. Upstairs they used reason, to explain; downstairs we played, to experience. Upstairs was meaning; downstairs was mystery.

The Creator of the Universe fashions order out of chaos, makes light and darkness, and shapes land and sea out of the void. He makes playmates (birds, animals, insects) and plants to feed them. Then comes the great surprise: human life, made out of clay in creation's playroom.

Unlike the animals, people can name their own creations— they have language. Words give Adam and Eve an ability to bond, to teach, and to learn. Or to wound, deceive, and betray.

Humans also have the unique ability to experience awe over creation. Awareness of magnificence is itself a gift: we're blessed even by our awareness of the blessing.

In biblical times, to know someone's name was to understand his essence. Today we ask, "What do you do?" (or worse, "What does your husband do?" or worst of all, "What does your ex-husband do?") to probe what we think is essential. A child names her creations to give them being. Creating her own kingdom delights extends her capacity for wonder.

The "adults" lead us upstairs too soon, out of our world of mystery. Upstairs, imagination is manufactured—video games, movies, TV, computer friendships—but something is always missing when we rely on other people's images. When we're not engaged in our own creation, we forfeit awe and forget reverence.

My daughter Beth said that little David, then three, had an imaginary friend, Robert. He was adamant that Robert "really" said and did certain things. Hearing about David's pretend companion took me back to the magic of my old basement kingdom.

I bought a children's book with an accompanying package of postcards about the characters. I sent the book to David with a card signed "Your secret pal, Robert." Later, "Robert" began sending David the postcards.

When David turned four and came to visit, we took a walk. Curious that he hadn't mentioned his fantasy friend, I asked, "How's Robert?"

"I haven't seen him for a long time," David said.

Uh-oh, Robert died. I am left uneasy, wondering, Why was I so tempted to enter into my grandchild's story? Did I terminate David's fantasy because I've forgotten how, or become too lazy, to create my own? Shouldn't I have known the futility of trying to appropriate a child's truth?

Our History of Hope

The years and miles have taken their toll on Momma's hope chest.

THIRD THURSDAY

The LORD calls you back,
like a wife forsaken and grieved in spirit,
A wife married in youth and then cast off,
says your God.
For a brief moment I abandoned you,
but with great tenderness I will take you back.
—Isaiah 54:6–7

My mother played with dolls until she was fifteen; she got her first period at seventeen. Long before that she was given a hope chest. Childhood lasted longer then, though responsibilities often came earlier. In Momma's day, a girl's hope began—officially—at age twelve. That was when most girls started to pack away treasures for their adult (synonymous then with "married") life.

Almost fifty years after she got it, Momma shipped her hope chest, fully stocked, to me. "It's all yours now," she warned in that "good riddance" tone of hers. I held the phone, imagining Momma's tight-lipped glare when she used to threaten me: "Someday you'll have a spiteful, sassy daughter just like you, and *then you'll know.* . . ." Even as a child I knew that she wasn't just warning me about a mother's frustrations; she hinted at a wife's struggles. A woman's.

But we weren't arguing now. I was the only daughter then with both a house and kids, and she needed to get rid of that chest. For whatever reason, Momma's hope, along with my parents' lives, seemed to be running on empty that year.

My hope ran out four years later; divorce meant that my life and my illusions required smaller quarters now *("then you'll know . . .")*. I shipped the chest to the only sister with basement storage space. It was still loaded with Great-Grandma Topliff's quilts, Grandma Miller's afghans, Momma's sterling silver packed in flannel. The heirlooms brought to mind the framed sampler that hung in the breakfast nook of my youth. Momma had made it as a girl, no doubt for her hope chest. "The Blessing of the House Is Contentment," it had proclaimed, before cross-stitching became crewel. The old chest seemed like a coffin for our family's hopes, cedar-lined to postpone the inevitable decay. I buried it in Kathleen's basement for the next decade.

During those years, the heirlooms seemed like an albatross, even entombed as they were in another state. Dare I thrust them on my own children in the future? A girlfriend cheerfully assured me I'd want to someday.

Why is other people's optimism so irritating when we're in the darkness? Because we see it as false hope? Or because we don't (and we fear that only our own hopes were false)? The landscape of change is shadowy, ominous. You find yourself lost in the dark woods, like Gretel. You entered relying on Hansel to be there holding your hand, when what you really needed was a scarecrow to preserve the trail back to daylight. Where's Hansel now? What happened to that trusty trail of bread crumbs showing you the way home?

Exile is the classic biblical punishment. God banishes Adam and Eve from the Garden, then sends their murderous son, Cain, to wander the earth. Noah begins a second race, whose punishment also becomes dispersal from their homeland. Isaiah consoles an exile-weary people: God, whose face is hidden, is found to have an enduring love for us, he says. Even God is bound to a place and a people; even God can get homesick.

Does God test me to learn something about me? Or so I can learn about myself? Self-knowledge, character, and strength are certainly gained by dealing with the test, by merely surviving it. But the stories of the heavily tested—Abraham, Job, Jesus— suggest something more: that an ultimate experience with the Divine is a possible outcome of suffering, that exile might lead me to Grace, Love, and Truth. Home.

Isaiah sounds maternal, echoing Momma's encouragement and solace throughout my life: "You can do it." "It could be worse." "Think of all you can be grateful for." Even exile can end in new life, their voices promise.

The trauma of exile makes me overlook the price that needs to be paid to stay in paradise. Innocence is gone, but it is better to know good from evil. Then, too, one must usually experience the shock of being transplanted from a sheltered garden in order to bloom.

Years later, I set down roots in a new city and reclaimed the old knotty pine chest. It arrived scratched and stained, a huge crack in one foot, though the contents were perfectly preserved.

Good years returned. My parents eventually celebrated their sixty-sixth anniversary. Cousin Richard, a widower, married at age fifty-seven and had children. I removed some of our grand-mother's handiwork from the chest and gave it to Richard for his three daughters. My children were coming of age. Momma and I became the spectator-commentators observing the next generation of our women, noting their illusions or lack of them, concerned with what psychic and material furnishings we might reliably equip their lives.

One year I sent some old furniture to one of my daugh-ters. After the truck pulled away, I realized I'd forgotten to have the driver load Momma's hope chest. I was getting new furniture, and Beth, a single mom with three sons, could probably have used the chest as a coffee table or at the foot of a bed. Perhaps my forgetfulness signaled a new comfort at being custodian of the chest and all it represents.

I'm content now to keep it until the next generation claims it. Most of the time I don't even notice the old broken-footed chest in our glass-walled city apartment. When I do, it reminds me of how skewed are hope's classic images. Hope doesn't really "burst forth" or "spring eternal." Not cultivated, it withers, I have learned. Banished, it reseeds in more hospitable soil. When I dared to beckon hope back, it didn't "soar" or "flood." It limped toward me like a neglected old mutt. But this bedraggled hound is a pointer, my sore-footed but trusty guide out of the wilderness.

Our family has learned to bequeath hope without calling the moving van, but the years and miles have taken their toll. It rests now in a little-used corner, our women's history of hope: contradictory, broken, wary, but sturdier than it looks.

Just like us.

Dog-Day Blessings

In blighted neighborhoods, nursing homes, and prisons—as in our family—reverence and harmony are cultivated along with lawns and gardens.

THIRD FRIDAY

The earth has yielded its harvest;
God, our God, blesses us.

—*Psalm 67:7*

My children talk about their lawns now. In Kansas they're raking, mulching, building the compost pile, and those in Georgia aerate, thatch, and seed in late fall. I—who don't own any grass and who once paved our backyard with maintenance-free green concrete—am grateful. Conversations with or about the kids no longer jangle my nerves like alarm bells, setting off both adrenaline and the counter call to keep calm.

Poison control centers, assistant principals, and ER physicians counsel other parents now, but certain phrases from those earlier days occasionally explode into my memory as I enjoy today's pastoral exchanges. I remember and am thankful that my children are grown and that I am so post-traumatically blessed.

Blue fescue is the superior grass in red-clay country, my Atlanta children claim, while Beth and her boys report that zoysia is taking over their lawn in Prairie Village, Kansas. When any yard is zoysia sodded, the zoysia creeps and blows into other yards, eventually carpeting whole subdivisions with its artificial-turfish sheen. Zoysia can't be stopped. It must be accepted, virtues and drawbacks alike, the way parents accept children who eventually outgrow them and take over the house, onetime shoots now matured into specimens unlike anything they'd imagined back when having a baby seemed like a good idea.

Zoysia is ugly in spring because it requires several days over seventy degrees to turn green. When the snow melts and reveals its greenery, my Kansans welcome their old grass. But they are dismayed to see its fresh emerald color splotched with straw-colored zoysia patches larger than last year, like that disease in which dark-skinned people lose pigmentation. Eventually summer's heat burns the old grass brown and drains my daughter's appetite for yard work; then she appreciates her outlandishly colorful (it's a suggestive, almost metallic green) zoysia. Along with overtaking less hardy varieties, it chokes out weeds as well. Such dog-day blessings are not to be sniffed at.

And I remember: "We'll have to do skin grafting on your baby. The boiling water made that cotton shirt stick, and when you yanked the shirt off, you pulled his skin with it. . . ."

My children also talk about their gardens. Brian and his wife, Arlene, both chefs, have brought their herbs indoors. They write that their laundry room provides perfect conditions for growing morel mushrooms—on top of the dryer.

And I remember: "Stir a tablespoon of flour into a glass of milk and make him drink that. But hurry. Have him drink it as you drive to the ER. We'll alert the hospital you're on the way. . . . His sister gave this to other children in your neighborhood? Bring in every child; one teaspoon is a lethal dose for adults. . . ."

Rabbits raid the Kansas plot; in Atlanta, Meredith battles a vole. Squirrels plague everyone, and nothing daunts them. Planting onions, marigolds, or other strong-smelling plants along the perimeter doesn't work, nor does sprinkling pepper, mothballs, or coyote urine. They scamper over a fake owl, laugh at scarecrows. Why can't any of my gardeners outwit a squirrel?

And I remember: "Your child is not working up to potential, and we're seeing a major attitude problem. . . ."

Beth puts 255 miles on her car a week, driving her sons to three different schools, ball practice, and youth groups. So I'm surprised when she phones to say she and the boys will adopt a boulevard plot next spring. They've volunteered to plant and tend its grass, flowers, and fountain, along with their own lawn and garden. I look out the window at my city vista of concrete and glass and ask, "Don't you have enough to care for already?"

And I remember: "You don't understand, Mom. You're always trying to get me to be just like you. . . ."

My children remind me of nature's hardy, variegated beauty: surviving and thriving. They teach me about plant-eating insects and insect-eating plants, morning glories and moonflowers, devil's guts and angel's trumpets, cupid's darts and fairy thimbles. Biblical stories are recalled in plants, ancient and merely old: Our Lady's gloves, Solomon's seal, a crown of many thorns, marigolds ("Mary's gold"), Saint Peter's keys, and Saint-John's-wort (named for John the Baptist, today's herbal antidepressant was used by medieval monks to treat sore throats). I smile, recalling a neighbor from long ago whose attorney sent a letter threatening to sue if my then-eight-year-old climbed his pear tree again. That cranky man is long gone from the old neighborhood. We are too. The pear tree remains.

And I remember: "This is Officer Clark from the Eighth District police station. . . ."

My children are closer to God in their gardens than anywhere else on earth. Their intuitive appreciation of our family and Judeo-Christian heritage—their love of what comes out of the earth—is keener than mine. Too far away, I encounter fruit of the land only as produce: by the pound, clean, waxed, and shrink-wrapped.

Like the psalmist, gardeners link divine justice and salvation to the place where "the earth has yielded its harvest; / [and] God . . . blesses us" (Ps. 67:7). The Creator is the first gardener. God's voice resonates there.

Two of my children confess to liking graveyards, and I admit, too, to spending time in cemeteries whose inhabitants are strangers. Perhaps my children can more easily explain this preoccupation since home gardens are ancient burial places. Jesus, too, is buried in a garden.

Jesus also prays, suffers, is betrayed and denied in a garden. At the empty tomb, Mary Magdalene mistakes Jesus for a gardener, then, recognizing her mistake, calls him rabbi. "Don't cling to me," he replies. Indicating she is no longer his student, Jesus commissions her to be his proclaimer. Now that his hour has come, so has hers. Magdalene is empowered in the garden.

Through my children's eyes I now see gardens as places of enchantment, mystery, and healing. I'm discovering newly planted church plots and peace gardens. A nearby retreat house is landscaping a maze of shrubbery to be used as a meditation path. In blighted neighborhoods, nursing homes, and prisons— as in our family—pacifism, reverence, harmony, and gratitude are cultivated along with lawns, flowers, vegetables, and herbs.

Eden remains the home from which we all went out and which we continually strive to reclaim.

My sons have kept birds since they were teenagers, an integral avocation for both. On her days off from work at a large nursery, Ann Marie helps my son David at Calentures, the shop they've opened to sell lawn art. He creates unique birdcages, reproduces architectural artifacts, and scours the country for one-of-a-kind concrete statuary. Some of his ornate pieces weigh twelve hundred pounds.

To get ready to host David and Ann Marie's April wedding, Meredith and her husband, David, began work on their yard—and their next-door neighbor's so it would look good too—in February. It took eight weekends and many evenings to make the landscape as beautiful as they envisioned. The other siblings and nephews came early to join this labor of love, potting, pruning, setting up tents on the front lawn, and erecting the wedding canopy in back. The bride and groom, who call seventeen pet birds by name, had a "birds of a feather" ceremony under the trees.

As music signaled the bride's appearance, all turned to see Ann Marie, floating down the stepping-stones in white silk, surrounded by greenery and blossoms of every color. Those tempted to choke up at such a heavenly scene burst into smiles and exchanged glances as she passed. Approaching the grove where my son awaited, Ann Marie walked by where I stood, and I too saw the lovely surprise in my children's garden: the bride was wearing wings.

Death-Ready Drawers

*Our great-grandmothers called the obsession to clean
before traveling "getting your drawers death-ready."*

FOURTH SUNDAY

Mary set out and traveled to the hill country in haste to a town of Judah, where she entered the house of Zechariah and greeted Elizabeth. When Elizabeth heard Mary's greeting, the infant leaped in her womb, and Elizabeth, filled with the holy Spirit, cried out in a loud voice.

—Luke 1:39–42

Before leaving town, the women in our family always have a fit of spring-cleaning, no matter what season it is. My friend Margot reports the same trait in her foremothers, though she herself would rather move than clean. ("Cleaning is dreary and lonely, but when you move, your friends all come to help.") Our great-grandmas called the obsession to clean before traveling "getting your drawers death-ready."

For Momma, serious cleaning always involved ladders. She'd be up high, removing prisms from the ceiling fixtures to give them a good wash and a vinegar rinse. Our handyman, Mr. Bogey, would be on another ladder rubbing down the wallpaper with a pink puttylike glob. He'd swipe light stripes on the paper, ceiling to floor, then knead the dirty putty back into the clean. By the time the putty was grimy and the flowers popped out on the walls again, we were pulling out of the driveway to visit the relatives in Perry, Iowa.

The men think it's crazy to equate leaving home with dying, but they are used to the way we start vacations exhausted from cleaning out closets and scrubbing cupboards. "Suppose you do die before you get back home, in spite of evidence to the contrary," my son David might say. "Why should you care about a clean house if you're going to be dead?" But our need to clean house before a journey is innate; arguing about it is like trying to persuade geese it would be more logical to live down south in the first place.

Margot adds that we don't clean house just to save our families all that work in case we never return. We do it to get rid of our secrets. But that's another story.

Some women who clean obsessively before traveling swear they never do housework at any other time. We claim we like returning to an orderly house, but I suspect there's more to it. Leaving home triggers powerful and primordial associations, and some of them are troubling.

Momma doesn't travel anymore. It's just too much trouble to leave her retirement community. Death is close enough there anyway, and her drawers are as ready as they're ever going to be. The rest of us understand.

Before the Nativity, everyone is leaving home. The whole world is in motion; babies leap in the womb; there is even movement in the spirit world. Zechariah goes to the temple, where an angel tells him that he and Elizabeth will have a son in their old age.

Time also becomes elastic as the present is kneaded into the past: their son, John, will have the spirit and power of the ancient Elijah. The angel goes to tell Mary that she'll also have a child, which leads Mary to travel to her cousin Elizabeth. The child John goes out into the desert; Joseph and Mary journey to Beth-

lehem; the angel comes to tell shepherds; Herod sends the wise
men out to find the child. Everyone is on a journey, troubled
and fearful, yet full of great expectation.

A child is born, and all creation is forever changed.

We also went on a cleaning binge right before childbirth. (Of course, a five- or six-day trip to the hospital was involved when I gave birth.) Our pregnancy cleaning binge predicted labor within twenty-four hours. Would anything other than a bred-in-the-bone compulsion make us choose to enter labor in a state of exhaustion?

Some of our women still do it before childbirth, even in this day of drive-by deliveries. We say it's because we won't be up to cleaning house for some time after the birth, but "death readiness" is also at work, consciously or not. On some level, we know that the woman who leaves home in labor is never coming back from the hospital. She's leaving to be kneaded into someone new, like Mr. Bogey's putty.

The world is so vividly fresh as she embarks on that indelible journey that she will tell the child, decades later, what she ate for supper that night, what was on the news, who said what in the delivery room. The woman who returns with a child in her arms is someone else. The new mother has also just given birth to the woman she's going to become.

Grown-up Lies

*Kathleen and me with Mrs. Billings, before she
conspired with our parents against us.*

December 8, Immaculate Conception

The man called his wife Eve, because she became the mother of all the living.

—Genesis 3:20

When I remember that day with my mother, my sister Kathleen, and our next-door neighbor Mrs. Billings, it's 1942 again, and I am four years old:

"You girls get to go to the hospital tomorrow, where Daddy works." Momma is talking with someone else's voice. Her smile is too big.

"What for?" I ask.

"Mrs. Billings is going with us. We're going so early that you girls can wear your pajamas." I wish Momma would quit saying things with that voice.

"Why?" Kathleen says. I'm glad she asks. She's older.

"She was a nurse once," Momma says.

What does that mean?

"Daddy says they give you ice cream." Momma makes her eyes round in a way that doesn't look like her.

When we get there, a long line of mothers and children goes all the way down the block. I ask why all these people are in front of the hospital. "Because they have to get everything done before polio season," Momma says. We go in the back of the hospital. I'm glad I don't have to stand out on the sidewalk in my pajamas.

I am scared when I see the needle. The nurse rubs my bottom with wet cotton that smells like the dentist's office. I am scared, but I hold my breath and don't cry when she gives me the shot. I get more scared when they leave me alone with Mrs. Billings. I hate having her by my bed, smelling like lilac bushes and reading me a dumb storybook. Where did Momma and Kathleen go without me? A man comes in and puts me on a cart and wheels me down a hall, maybe to where they are.

Now a lot of strangers in masks look down on me. A voice asks can I count to twenty. Do they think I'm a baby?

" . . . five, six, seven, eight, . . ." My face is covered with the smell of a filling station, and that roaring sound makes everything go black.

I open my eyes and see Mrs. Billings's face. She puts a wet cloth on my forehead. I start to cry, but my throat makes me stop. It burns and I can't swallow. Did I get polio?

There's Momma by the other bed. She holds the bowl for Kathleen. Kathleen throws up blood. Momma says, "Ohhh, honey." Kathleen looks at me.

They knew, our eyes say to each other. Her face twists to cry. Her face stops, and I know her throat feels like a bad skinned knee too, and she is trying not to move. My tears want to come too, but I have to stop them. It all hurts too much. They knew. Momma tries to give Kathleen ice cream, and Mrs. Billings is standing with a cup and a flat wooden spoon asking do I want some. But I won't look at her. I watch Kathleen turn her face away from the ice cream. I do that too.

It was the first time the grown-ups lied to us, and it hurt too much to cry.

Adam and Eve learn about good and evil, shame and death, all in one bite. Now they'll have to make millions of choices, most of which will distract them from the awful knowledge that they're going to die. It's a lot to swallow, this apple.

Betrayal comes quickly. "She made me do it," says Adam.

"No, no," Eve says. "It was that snake."

The first mother becomes the mother of Cain, who eventually kills his brother. First he plays dumb: "Am I my brother's keeper?" He probably then tries blame: "What can you expect from such parents?"

God has none of it. He punishes Cain with perpetual homelessness. So we all begin.

"Lord, I know who is to blame for my sins," I vow, "and I will not perpetrate such wrongs on my children." I hope to break the chain of errors and betrayals, to start a healthy new generation in my family and in the world.

My own attempts also bring shame, but humility too, and with that a better hope: to reenter the human race through forgiveness. I hope to begin with me. It's a never-ending quest.

Momma said, "The truth hurts" so often to me as a child that I wondered about and feared learning whatever terrible truths she knew. The nuns then told me that Jesus said, "I am the Truth" and that Truth is beautiful. Even then I suspected Momma's mantra was the one I should count on.

Years later, I tell my children, "This is just what they call a separation. Daddy and I are going to live apart for a little while." Beth's eyes well up, and she says, "Are you getting a divorce?" Tears spill down Beth's cheeks, and I know the three younger ones will take their cue from her. She's eleven.

I hug them and say firmly, "No, don't worry. Daddy and I will never get a divorce," hoping it is true. It turns out not to be.

Momma's lifelong lesson becomes mine too, only Momma gave me the condensed version. My children learn the full text: the truth hurts, but denying the truth hurts even more.

Later my avoidance of truth became apparent when I think of that day with my nine-year-old grandson Matthew.

"Grandma Carol, do you think if Uncle George knew that I would be born someday that he would have taken better care of his old baseball cards—Joe DiMaggio, Mickey Mantle, and all those valuable ones?"

"Honey, all the kids in my day had those cards, even Kathleen and me. Everyone's mother eventually threw them away, or they got lost. Nobody knew they'd become so valuable."

"Who's your favorite?" He loves for me to name the old players who cost hundreds.

"My favorite's Roger Maris, but he came along long after I quit collecting. Your aunt Kathleen liked Yogi Berra. Who are you looking for now?" His mother, my daughter Beth, has told him he can't ask me to buy him trading cards, but he likes to let me know his special wish list.

"In the packs I collect Topps and Upper Deck. But for some players I collect all the brands. My best ones are Nolan Ryan and Bo Jackson. Bo's both baseball and football. Joe Montana's my favorite football card, and my favorite basketballs are Michael Jordan and Magic Johnson. Do you want me to write these out for you?"

"Please. Then if a special occasion comes, I'll have your list." It's our way to get around his mother's rule without actually breaking it. Matt's eagerly making a list when he stops and asks, "Grandma, will I get AIDS?"

I see that he's just written Magic Johnson's name.

"Oh, heavens no, Matt." I laugh nervously.

"Did you know Magic got it?"

"Yes, that's very sad. But kids don't have to worry about

AIDS." I lift his album from the coffee table and pat the place next to me on the sofa, trying to get him to talk about his other favorite players. He doesn't move.

"But how did Magic get it?"

"Well, he led a kind of wild life. Honey, you don't get AIDS from sharing a drinking glass or other things that kids do." I flip to the other players. "Oh, here's a George Brett."

"How old do you have to be to get AIDS?" he asks. Such an intense child, just like his mother was, not easily sidetracked. I rise to get the TV clicker.

"Matt, by the time you're that age they'll have a cure. President Bush is working on it right now." Or at least that's what they claim. I return to the sofa and click on Nickelodeon. *My Three Sons* comes on in black and white. He comes to sit by me. I hug him and whisper, "Don't worry about it, honey," hoping he's heard enough.

Did I tell him enough to reassure him, or did he just give in to my unwillingness to tell children unpleasant truths? Did I protect myself at his expense? Will he still worry about getting AIDS?

I decide to tell his mother about Matt's AIDS worries. She—my daughter Beth—was so much like Matt, a firstborn child who watched the adult world and wanted grown-up knowledge so young. Beth who forgives my ineptness at confronting hurtful truths. Still.

What Is Left Behind

This 1950 photo of Grandma and me with W. K. Kellogg, the cereal man, was taken with an amazing new invention, the Polaroid camera.

DECEMBER 17

Jacob called his sons and said: "Gather around, that I may tell you what is to happen to you in days to come."

—Genesis 49:1

Grandma Miller took me with her to Battle Creek, Michigan, to see cereal magnate W. K. Kellogg, at age ninety, one last time. That summer of 1950, I was eleven. My grandparents had just celebrated their fiftieth anniversary, a victory, I later learned, over Kellogg's attempt to prevent their marriage.

Back in 1900, Grandma refused Kellogg's offer of a trip to Europe if she wouldn't marry Grandpa. For the next fifty years until his death, W. K. pretended Grandpa didn't exist, even when they lived under the same roof.

My grandparents met each other and the Kelloggs in Michigan when they were all Seventh-day Adventists. In the prior century, W. K.'s father had been a believer in the visions of Ellen G. White, one of the SDA founders. Sister White, who preached abstinence from alcohol, caffeine, and meat, urged the establishment of a spa in Battle Creek. W. K.'s older brother, John, became the spa's administrator when he graduated from medical school.

Dr. John was a marketing genius with bizarre health theories: Advocating a roughage-free diet (John removed the hulls from beans), he took a daily enema. Some historians claim he believed sex was unhealthy and never consummated his long marriage. Eventually he gained control of the spa and its sales of cornflakes, a tasteless cereal he'd devised. Dr. John promoted the spa as a sanitarium and attracted famous guests like John D. Rockefeller, Henry Ford, William Jennings Bryan, Eleanor Roosevelt, and Amelia Earhart.

Meanwhile, Grandma had become a companion to W. K. Kellogg's frail wife and governess for their children. Aware of tension between the brothers, her sympathies were with W. K. She called Dr. John "supercilious, an eccentric quack." In 1955, at their request, Grandma wrote the Kellogg biographers about her life with the family, telling them that W. K.'s wife suffered "acute indigestion from eating [her brother-in-law's meat substitutes] Bromose, Protose, Nutose, Granose, Mock Turkey, mock-this and that."

Grandma served unofficially as peacemaker in W. K.'s house. She describes a difficult bunch: the "austere, dictatorial" W. K. and his sickly wife; their oldest boy, an "artistic dreamer" who irritated his dad; a younger "rebellious, problem son" whom W. K. favored; and "a sweet but slow" daughter.

After they married, Grandpa moved into Grandma's room in the Kellogg mansion. "Mr. Kellogg never talked to [my husband], ever," Grandma writes. "He was never included in the family circle although I was. . . . Mr. K. was a man of deep prejudice and my husband married me against his wishes. . . . My husband was understanding, he would always say, 'Go with the family, do as Mr. Kellogg wants.'" But after a few months, my grandparents moved to Iowa.

The Kellogg brothers soon became estranged. W. K. looked back on those events in a letter to Grandma in which he claimed that after twenty-five years of working for John he'd given notice he would "start something of [his] own." When Dr. John returned from Europe in 1906, he found W. K. had added refined sugar to the cornflakes. The new cereal was a hit with consumers and a horror to his health-food-fundamentalist brother. It didn't matter. W. K. had bought up all the company's controlling stock.

Until our trip, Grandma hadn't seen W. K. again for fifty years, but they wrote. When my grandparents' youngest son died at age ten, W. K. sent a letter, sharing the grief he'd known when his own younger "favorite" son died. A quarter century later, when W. K. received Grandma's condolences on his older son's death, he phoned, begging her to come. Once again, Grandpa told her to go to Mr. Kellogg, not minding that the invitation had excluded him. She took me along to visit the old man, who was in his last days and sightless.

The dying Jacob's eyesight is gone, but he can see what matters. W. K. is more afflicted. Both end a long life as wealthy men. Jacob's children and grandchildren attend his deathbed. Only servants are at W. K.'s.

Jacob's jealous sons are known for plotting against each other, vying for their father's approval. Younger sons triumph, often by devious means, not unlike the Kellogg brothers.

Jacob's final words are honest. The time for pretense has run out. The sins of his children are recounted, the disappointments listed. The scoundrels are forgiven and blessed along with the worthy. Forgiveness is vital in families where disloyalty cuts deep and its scars last long. Without healing, bitterness becomes a poisonous legacy, tainting family members not yet born.

Jacob understands family: the father must love them all. Chosen ones from Abraham to Jacob open the door through twenty-eight generations to the birth of Christ, when everyone can be priest and prophet. Neither Jew nor Greek, male nor female is barred from inheriting Grace.

W. K. lost sight of the ancient lessons. My grandfather was to leave a different legacy.

I remember the Seeing Eye dog, the tour of the cereal factory, the Kellogg estate on Lake Michigan where I saw television for the first time. Mr. Kellogg was kind to me, but he revealed his despair to Grandma. Though both had abandoned Adventism, he said that "Christianity is lost"; she had hope it might enrich the world. When Grandma asked why his daughter wasn't there to see her, W. K. said, "She'd have come if I'd have paid for the trip." The old man's harshness toward his last living child, the sweet daughter, pained Grandma, who wrote:

"[Our] opinions after fifty years were aeons apart, religion, politics—there was no common ground. . . . In the old days, if our ideas differed, we would have a lively discussion; now if I expressed myself he gave a curt [reply], and he could be the curtest of any human. My [condolence] letter had seemed like old times, so he had reached out to me for comfort in his darkest hour, and I had failed [to comfort him]. He and I . . . were tongue tied. He was blind, not only to face and figure, but to thoughts and understanding."

Meanwhile, Grandpa wrote, encouraging us to visit his relatives nearby: "I would like the Michigan folks to see how well you have borne up for over fifty years of putting up with one of the Miller boys, and I also want folks there to see the 'classy' grandchild we have."

Grandpa typed long letters full of strikeovers on his old manual machine, silly stories and encouragement, whenever I was away. He'd quote "Young men for war, but old men for counsel" before launching thoughts on kindness, forgiveness, and family. Once he apologized for "a little preaching so my lovable Granddaughter Carol may . . . learn . . . that life is not all getting, but is best and worthwhile when giving has its place."

Like W. K., Grandpa outlived his spouse and all but one child. After losing Grandma and his older son within three months, my grief-stricken grandpa was no longer the exuberant man "with verbal diarrhea" he had once been. Momma, the only survivor of his four children, claims he died of a broken heart.

Long before that, he'd written me, "As I think of being blessed with [my family] I forget about . . . the price that was paid for these children. . . . I am convinced that if just one child were to live after mother and I are gone he or she would be worth a million times what they all cost [in sacrifice and concern]." At his hour of death, he'd exhausted his God-given energies wisely, passionately, lovingly. His name evokes cherished memories among his seven grandchildren.

W. K. Kellogg's name is known to millions; it evokes breakfast cereal. He'd once written Grandma that "too much money" was more often a source of "galling experiences" than of happiness. It remained so to the end.

He died a few months after Grandma and I visited. Seven years earlier, his brother John had tried to reconcile. Servants who had once prevented Grandma from seeing W. K. on an earlier unannounced visit withheld his brother's letter from W. K. Now his older brother was dead, W. K. was on his deathbed, and one servant finally revealed that Dr. John had offered to patch up their differences years ago.

"My goodness, why didn't someone tell me before this?" W. K. asked.

Emmanuel's Promise

We know Joseph only through his dreams,
but they are spectacular.

December 18

*The angel of the Lord appeared to him in a dream and said,
"Joseph, son of David, do not be afraid to take Mary your
wife into your home."*

—Matthew 1:20

One of the advantages of marriage is that you wake up next to someone to tell your dream to while it still has you in its grip. Some dreams seem to be nothing more than "garbage out" overflow of brain activity. Others are so mysterious and emotion-packed they challenge us to decode their message.

Physiological studies show great activity during sleep, as dreams stimulate increased heart and adrenaline rates. Perhaps the notion that someone dies peacefully in her sleep is a myth. The deceased was probably having a vivid dream.

A bizarre Silly Putty substance—but with the endless reach of the cartoon Plastic Man's arms—figures often in my nightmares. I dream that this disgusting material is coming out of my mouth, endlessly, like a sticky magician's scarf. I'm trying to hide my embarrassing regurgitation from onlookers as I pull, pull to get rid of it. But it just keeps coming. In my last dream, broken glass was embedded in the stretchy stuff. I've noticed this dream occurs either before or after a potentially touchy personal encounter. I fear what might come out of my mouth, that I might say something to increase, rather than resolve, the tension.

The communion of saints surely includes the appearance of deceased loved ones in dreams. My husband, Stan, has dreamt of a long conversation with his father (then dead over twenty years) about their business, which his dad had founded. The dream was comforting: Stan envisioned sharing stories with one perfectly suited to appreciate them.

Dream activity—like intuition—seems to involve an artistic, problem-solving, or prophetic unconscious self that commands attention. College test taking is an occasional nightmare. I'm either lost and can't find the exam room or don't have a pencil. The test is timed; the clock is ticking; and I'm failing before I can get started. My friend Velma from college days e-mailed me her version of it: "Last night I dreamed you and I went off to college again. We were our present ages and were going to live in the dorm, but I was upset because I couldn't find the stupid dorm! I felt depressed about being in college again, but you said, 'There's one really good thing about this college.' But then my dream ended, so I have no idea what that might be."

This common dream, I've learned, occurs when the dreamer is faced with a challenge or decision. Oddly, it usually appears long after, not during, student days. Velma seemed to want me to supply what I was going to say in her dream, and it was tempting to guess at it, but I had to respond that the answer resided within her, not me.

Some visions occur when we are awake, or seem to be. Consider Martin Luther King Jr.'s famous "I Have a Dream" speech. He may have been using "dream" figuratively—to mean his hope for a peaceful America, where people are judged only on the content of their character—but that visionary speech is laced with the Hebrew Bible's images of waters of the Promised Land, waters of justice and streams of righteousness, and crooked places made straight.

He delivered variations on his "dream" speech over the years and in 1968 added a talk with the Almighty about mortality. King told God, "If you allow me to live just a few years in the second half of the twentieth century, I will be happy." He concluded that rousing apocalyptic sermon: "Like anybody, I would like to live a long life. Longevity has its place. But I'm not concerned about that now. I just want to do God's will. And he's allowed me to go up to the mountain. . . . And I've seen the promised land. I may not get there with you. But . . . I'm happy, tonight. Mine eyes have seen the glory of the coming of the Lord." The next morning he was assassinated.

It can be difficult to determine what role the unconscious dream state plays in such visions. When our daughter Linda was expecting her first child, she believed she was carrying a boy, though she declined to have the doctor confirm it. One morning late in the pregnancy, she looked at treetops out her bedroom window and saw a girl child's face in the branches. She was about to wake her husband up to see the face, but because she was in that twilight state between dreams and wakefulness, she wondered if she'd just been dreaming and looked again. The little girl's face she'd just seen was gone. She guessed she'd been dreaming seconds before, but the vivid image remained with Linda, and she became certain she was carrying a girl. "It reminded me of the poster girl for *Les Miz*," she later told her husband, Al. Linda never forgot that face. Now, over two years later, she sees it daily; Isabel, the daughter she gave birth to, has finally grown into that girl Linda saw in the trees.

If Shakespeare were writing today, his editor would delete all those dream scenes. Modern audiences wouldn't buy plots hinging on the dead communicating with the living or the foreshadowing of events in dreams. We can't sell the "we are such stuff as dreams are made of" idea today, editors would say. Yet while we don't encounter dreams in drama anymore, we encounter them at night. Even when their meaning is unclear, they can exert a hold so powerful that some meaning is implicit, if only it could be decoded. Dreamers are called beyond the waking world of time and space into deeper, more intricate and puzzling questions of who they are or how they're related to others and to the mystery of another fascinating dimension of reality.

> There are more things in heaven and earth,
>   Horatio,
> Than are dreamt of in your philosophy.
>
> —*Hamlet*

Because Joseph is a carpenter, many assume he is a simple man. He may just as well be an intellectual who teaches Jesus to read and write, a scholar whose Torah lessons enable the boy at twelve to dazzle the learned men in the temple. Little else is known about Joseph, other than the intimate stories in his dreams. They tell him he is to become the father of Emmanuel, the promise of God-with-us; they warn him to go to a strange land to protect the child from Herod; they notify him when it is safe to go to Galilee. His dreams reveal that God is with him, even before Jesus is. Maybe all dreams point to a human connection with Divine Mystery.

Such mystical events are common experiences in biblical lives. A constant perception of the unearthly is "natural" to the psalmists and prophets, whose dreams channel revelation. Ecclesiastes says that dreams "come with many cares" (5:2), which is true for Solomon, whose dreams grant him the ability to solve complex problems.

The Bible's great dreamers are Jacob and his son Joseph. Jacob's dream is also a promise that God is with him. Angels on a ladder indicate that the spot where he sleeps is sanctified, "the gateway to heaven" (Gen. 28:17). Jacob is told that the land he must leave will be his eventually and that he will be blessed with many descendants. Later, a dream tells Jacob to return to that land.

Joseph's brothers are so jealous of his early prophetic dreams of glory that they sell him into slavery. In exile, Joseph's ability to interpret Pharaoh's dreams saves him and puts him on the road to glory, ultimately saving his family too.

Then and now, dreams point to a reality beyond the visible, conscious, and self-centered. Kabbalists, saints, and sages claim to receive Wisdom directly from the Source. Their vision of God-with-us is as irrational and real as love, hope, memory, and awe. Padre Pio, the stigmatic monk, wrote:

"I cannot explain myself properly and any expression I use invariably falls short of the reality. All I can say is that the Lord penetrates into my soul without the slightest effort and suddenly the truth speaks of its own accord, without noise of words and without mental images."

In my nightmare, I'd been involved in a car accident and hurled out of my vehicle. The contents of both my purse and my internal organs had spilled onto the highway, intermingling and stuck in that familiar dream substance: a giant bubble-gummy wad. (This time it was coming, not from my mouth, but from my chest cavity.) Passersby who tried to pull out any item found it stuck to an expanding string of the pink gluey stuff. Great tension awaited the examining doctor's verdict there at the roadside. I longed for and feared his prognosis: "Am I going to live?" Finally he looked over the gory mess of my life and heart and belongings and announced, "This is going to be a very serious litigation."

I awakened suddenly, puzzled by the word "litigation," trying to place it in a medical context: ligature? concussion? tubal ligation? Ah, litigation, I remembered, is a legal term. Then I understood. My dream was telling me that as painful as my divorce was, I'd survive.

"Nightmares are poor dramatists because they have no third act," the English critic Max Beerbohm once said. "They dump you at the climax of terror." Nightmares may be frightening because they can be life-changing. They foreshadow the need to go into new territory (exile), to tackle problems the conscious mind wants to bury, to change. The prospect of writing the final acts of my own nightmares is both terrifying and thrilling.

A Mime Is a Terrible Thing to Waste

Overnight, Hurricane Andrew ripped away all that was familiar, then heaped new identities on Florida's children—"homeless," "hurricane victim," "new kid"— like rubble after the storm.

DECEMBER 19

As for the son [Samson] you will conceive and bear, no razor shall touch his head, for this boy is to be consecrated to God from the womb.

—Judges 13:5

[John] will drink neither wine nor strong drink. He will be filled with the holy Spirit even from his mother's womb.

—Luke 1:15

The principal led me through rows of "temporary" barracks that had long outlived that designation even before Hurricane Andrew gave them renewed purpose by blasting away every structure in Homestead, Florida. Like flying debris, Homestead's kids had been scattered all over the neighboring communities—wedged into already crowded schools.

I had responded to a plea from a *Miami Herald* columnist for volunteers in the now overcrowded schools, hoping there was some way I could be useful. I had been assigned to this low-income public school where traumatized Homestead kids had been plopped into the everyday-problem stew. Overnight everything familiar had been ripped from their lives. They'd lost their homes, schools, churches, friends, their identity. Alien labels—"homeless," "hurricane victims," "new kids"— were heaped on them now, like rubble after the storm.

I'd once helped my daughter's sixth-grade class publish a newsletter, but I had no in-class volunteer experience. I didn't have specific ideas of how I might help, but I came willing to provide office or in-class assistance as needed. After all, how hard could grammar school be?

The principal introduced me to Mrs. Rose, a very pregnant third-grade teacher whose eyes welled up when told I'd come three afternoons a week. "Thank you," she said quietly to the principal, and I sensed something else had passed between them. I feared this teacher presumed she was getting more than I could offer. Mrs. Rose might have been surprised to know I'd hadn't been in a third-grade classroom since I was a third grader, but there was no time to tell her. "Too little time" could have been the third-grade motto, I soon learned.

On the first day—and only then—she took time to give me a one-sentence summary of each of the six children assigned to my table. "Rosario is a Title-this, needs help with math." "Madelene is a Title-that, has reading problems." One haunted me: "Jason doesn't speak or do anything. We can't get any response from him. Just let him listen."

After the first week, my fear that Mrs. Rose overestimated my capabilities escalated to near panic when I found she had no time to explain anything. Oceans of administrative paperwork having to do with lunches and field trips had to be completed, along with the many daily lesson goals. Constant interruptions from the children, squawky messages over the intercom, inadequate supplies, lost textbooks—the challenges were ongoing. The Title-this and Title-that children (mysterious coded numbers for "has major problems," I guessed) assigned to my back-of-the-room table varied, and her general suggestion to "help them with incomplete assignments" confused me. How could I work with so many different incomplete assignments at once?

The kids liked to use times-table flash cards, so we usually did that as a group. Most knew their twos and fives and tens, so I'd throw in those "easy" ones along with the threes and fours that gave them trouble. I was pleased at all correct responses. I hesitated to interrupt the overwhelmed Mrs. Rose for all the answers I'd have needed to do anything else.

Even so, I felt useful. I was surprised that most kids, rather than feeling punished, liked to be assigned to my table. Perhaps they enjoyed the special attention. After a couple of weeks of times tables, though, I had a major question. I planned a way to shoot it to Mrs. Rose at the least disruptive time. Walking to the front of the room with some students going out to a special class, I veered over to the teacher for a hurried exchange:

"How far should third graders be able to go on their times tables?"

"Through twelve times twelve."

I was surprised, frightened, embarrassed. No wonder they liked being at my table! We'd accomplished nothing. Had I actually been holding them back? I needed to expect more, to assign each student multiples to master daily. I felt overwhelmed. These children needed more help than they were likely to get from a fumbling amateur like me. What would become of them? Could they catch up?

The occasional substitute teacher heightened my growing appreciation of Mrs. Rose's skills. One man yelled at the children all day, disrupting the class rather than controlling it, and leaving me with shattered nerves. I worried the class would have him when Mrs. Rose left to have the baby, since she was too far along to finish the semester.

I enjoyed the times my group joined the general class, especially on what I came to think of as "Florida flora and fauna" days. I got a break, admired Mrs. Rose's teaching skills, and learned about anhinga birds, saw grass, and cloud patterns. Mostly, though, I learned how demanding a teacher's day is. Every minute requires focused energy: she's allowed no daydreaming, no personal calls to alleviate tension, no relaxed moments, even—especially—on the playground or in the lunchroom. Such strain can make the most capable teacher short-tempered. Mrs. Rose exploded one hot, sticky afternoon after a story they'd read led her to ask, "Does anyone know what a mime is?"

Andre wasn't in my group, but he had often captured my attention. An antsy kid, his generous grin seemed wired to his jerky limbs. Now, Andre not only knew the answer, he could show it. He bolted out of his seat to enact a "mime trapped in a large box" routine, patting the sides, top, and corners of his imaginary container-prison. He was so good I imagined his shiny black face plastered with chalky mime makeup. He crouched and patted the perimeters of his "box," his expression frozen into a sweetly surprised mime face: raised eyebrows, wide eyes, lips pursed into an O. His performance enchanted me.

But not Mrs. Rose, whose frustrations from a muggy day with jittery children erupted loudly. "Andre! You know you're not allowed to jump out of your chair. Sit down." He complied quickly, but he'd noted my attention and my appreciation. Obediently folding his body into his seat like a stringed puppet, Andre looked back to meet my eyes and said, "A mime is a terrible thing to waste."

Children have gifted me with cherished moments that become keepsakes: the unexpectedness of a sudden peek into a child's view of the world or of me. It's a privilege to be included, merely to be there. The very surprise of it triggers joy.

Such rare epiphanies help parents and teachers get through all the rest: stress, fatigue, problems, and a sense of their own inadequacies. In the midst of parenting, I was seldom tempted to view my children—at least when they were awake—as revealers of the sacred. Later, looking back to those earlier years, I can better appreciate the magic that was always there.

Biblical accounts are also written after the event, which sometimes adds mythical qualities, perhaps making them even truer to the purpose of sacred stories. People who encounter God in the Bible are astonished, awed, grateful.

All births are miraculous, especially biblical ones. A blessing is given against great odds and the rules of nature. Angels announce that the Virgin Mary and barren women like Sarah, Hannah, and Elizabeth will conceive. Often the angels name the child, for the child's purpose and identity are already known to God. From the womb, the child is blessed. So blessed that these children grow to alter the very course of history and to sanctify the parent. "From now on will all ages call me blessed," Mary says (Luke 1:48).

Such stories satisfy a hunger for accounts of the mystery of life and death and creation. Ancient stories of children born to grateful and awe-filled parents pulse with the recognition of a mystical yet familiar truth. So do some of those magical, out-of-the-blue utterances of the children I have loved and lived with and those who have graced me with a once-upon-a-time, unforgettable moment, such as Andre.

Mrs. Rose hadn't heard Andre's pun; it had been intended just for me. She'd already resumed talking to the class. Andre had required nothing but my split second of delight. In one fluid motion, he had tossed me his giddy gift, seen that I'd relished it, then settled down. I stared at the back of his head, savoring the moment.

Andre showed me what the exhausted Mrs. Rose must have seen in that room: talent, intelligence, spirit, a great potential straining to burst through the stifling atmosphere. Andre, one of those Title-numbered kids in a world inhospitable to learning, to humor, to joy, mimed an angelic messenger. He would prevail, I felt. That eight-year-old artist, by pulling order out of chaos and beauty out of destruction, gave me hope for the other children too.

Grandma Says Yes

Like most young brides, Grandma Dorothy couldn't fully comprehend the vulnerability she had incurred when she said yes to Grandpa Wen.

December 20

"Hail, favored one! The Lord is with you." But she was greatly troubled at what was said and pondered what sort of greeting this might be. Then the angel said to her, "Do not be afraid, Mary."

—Luke 1:28–30

Grandma's *what?"* My son whooped into the phone he'd just answered. Brian's continued reactions to what he was hearing kept me at his side. "Aw-right!" "Wow!" "Great!" Grandma Dorothy, whose life was family and church, didn't usually generate such excitement. Had she won the lottery?

In a way, yes, as it turned out. It was the year that a national magazine ran a story about the slim chance of women remarrying. After age forty, the widely quoted article said, a woman has a greater chance of being on a hijacked airplane. So when Brian hung up and trumpeted, "Grandma's getting married!" it seemed as if—in her seventies—she'd beaten lottery-scale odds.

Brian told me some of the story; then different family members, including Grandma, filled me in on details. Charlie, a widower, joined Visitation Church in Grandma's old Des Moines neighborhood. The church had a high concentration of elderly parishioners, predominately female. Charlie must have been suddenly surrounded by eligible women, but he had his eye on only one. After Mass one Sunday, Charlie stopped Grandma on the church steps and invited her to brunch. Grandma told me she became unnerved after accepting his invitation, realizing she "hadn't said yes to a man in sixteen years!" She was shaken because she knew very well what saying yes can let you in for.

Her husband, Wen, had died just before his retirement. They'd been planning the future for years: outfitting a van, visiting grandchildren en route to seeing America. She was such a kid as a bride, she'd always said, that Wen used to scold her for swinging on the screen door. Her entire adult life had been spent married to Wen. Suddenly she was like the lone sock at the bottom of the dryer, without a mate, feeling useless. And terrified. She'd never worked outside the home where they'd raised five children. Her future was to have been with Wen. She endured a long and difficult bereavement.

Grandma remained mum about "keeping company" with Charlie for months. Keeping such a juicy secret proved a great feat in their small parish, which included Grandma's married daughter and many of her grandchildren. Grandma said that she feared it would be difficult for the grandchildren to imagine anyone beside her in "Grandpa's place." I didn't mention that the sixteen years since Grandpa's death was an entire childhood for many of the grandkids, that they would surely welcome her happiness now. I suspected that the one who had to adjust to the idea of another marriage was, of course, Grandma.

Charlie and his first wife had not had children, and I doubt Charlie felt he shouldn't reveal their courtship, though he honored Grandma's wishes. They surprised their young assistant pastor by enrolling in PreCana Conference, the Catholic marriage-preparation course, and Grandma made the priest vow not to tell anyone. Bursting to share the news in the parish, he later said that not spreading their good cheer had been his most difficult task as a priest.

Then Charlie gave Grandma a gift that demanded telling. He invited Grandma to go with him and a chaperone to see the pope in Montreal. Keeping her gentleman caller a secret from her children and friends was one thing, but she couldn't keep from them that she'd taken a bus all the way to Canada and seen the pope. So things moved swiftly.

With her permission, Charlie asked Grandma's oldest son, Ken, then in his fifties, to lunch where Charlie declared his intentions to marry Grandma and asked for Ken's blessing. Everyone, especially the twenty-six grandchildren, was eager to be a part of this happy occasion. The grandsons gave Charlie a bachelor dinner; the granddaughters threw a bridal shower for Grandma. Beloved family friends of almost sixty years were asked to be matron of honor and best man.

An elderly couple's wedding Mass is a triumph of hope and love: white hair, hearing aids, corsages, couples walking down the aisle with arms linked to steady their pace. A church packed with family and friends shared their happiness. At the wedding, the priest read the PreCana director's evaluation of Grandma and Charlie as candidates for marriage. She wrote that their wisdom and gratitude, obviously the result of strong first marriages, inspired the other couples. The young people in the course had been blessed by Grandma's and Charlie's participation.

On that day, I didn't think about the reason for Dorothy's secrecy while she contemplated marriage. She was deciding if she could bear widowhood again. The first time, when she was fifty-seven, entailed years of grieving. She was now seventy-two, and Charlie was several years older. She was not lonely;

her life was filled with her large family, many friends, and activities. The odds were overwhelming she'd suffer a devastating loss again if she married at this age. Could she survive such grief in her seventies or eighties?

When I was a child, the Annunciation story seemed to be about an angel bringing good news to a joyful, accepting Mary. I overlooked that Mary is deeply troubled and that the angel recognizes her reaction as fear.

Now I see beyond the Mary of the Magnificat, exquisite as that portrait is, calmly submitting to the angel's strange message. I suspect that Mary's emotional reaction to the news—to that which she was being asked to accept—would have gone something like this:

"Wait! Let me understand. You have told me that I, Mary, am singled out for God's favor. That the seed of Wisdom, Grace, Truth is to be planted in me?

"Don't go before you tell me this: How do I explain this to Joseph? To anyone? Have I just been given a blessing or a burden? Why do I fear that you bring me sorrow, along with all the rest of it? 'Don't be afraid,' you say! Then tell me: how can I not be afraid?"

But Mary says yes.

Pregnancy is often hopeful. It can also be traumatic. Mary runs to see Elizabeth, also pregnant, because sometimes only sisterhood can help a woman cope. She spends three months with Elizabeth, returning, presumably, steadied for her fate. Even this young, inexperienced girl senses that Love insists on a terrifying vulnerability, that when you love you will grieve. Elizabeth cannot tell her otherwise.

And it came to pass.

Her sister Mary told me of visiting Dorothy a few years after Wen died. Mary came into the kitchen quietly one morning and found Dorothy on her knees at the kitchen sink, apparently suddenly overcome with sadness, praying for strength. Leaving her alone with her sorrow, Mary backed out, haunted by this image of a widowhood she had not yet experienced and the reminder that grief keeps its own timetable.

Dorothy forced herself to banish such reminders once she said yes to Charlie. Every day during their marriage Charlie and Dorothy recited the ancient words—God's instructions for blessing one another—from the book of Numbers:

> The LORD bless you and keep you!
> The LORD let his face shine upon you, and be
>   gracious to you!
> The LORD look upon you kindly and give you
>   peace!   —6:24–26

Grandma said this blessing over Charlie about sixty seconds before he took his last breath. They had almost seven years together.

I worried about Grandma in this second widowhood, recalling her earlier trauma. I wrote asking how anyone gets through such grief in later life. I didn't say as much, but I also wondered, Was it wise to have said yes at such a vulnerable age?

She wrote back, "It was getting very difficult for Charlie to cope [with his infirmity] and difficult for me to see him go downhill so fast. He was critically ill, so [it was] a blessing to see him slip away so peacefully. I have so many memories to keep me happy . . . and wedding pictures of the two good men in my life. Charlie and I never forgot our first mates. . . . Between you and me, every night I spend a little time conversing with them both."

She could no longer keep up the house and yard, so she was moving into a retirement community. It was difficult leaving the home that Charlie and she had shared, but everyone in the new place seemed friendly, Dorothy reported. She intended to make the best of it. After her first widowhood, she got a job as a nurse's aide in the intensive care unit of a hospital. Caring for others had helped her heal. At the retirement home she looked forward to volunteering in the nursing-home wing.

While Grandma's second widowhood was surely no easier than her first one, she went into her late marriage fully aware of the price she would pay. She let me know, even as she grieved, that saying yes to Charlie had been a good decision. "I made up my mind I would be happy and remember the good times [when loss came]," she wrote.

And it came to pass that Grandma did just that for the next six years, until she died.

Momma's Enchanted Supper

George won the privilege of being the groom, but love still surprised the adults who tried to engineer it.

DECEMBER 21

*"O my dove in the clefts of the rock,
  in the secret recesses of the cliff,
Let me see you,
  let me hear your voice,
For your voice is sweet,
  and you are lovely."*

—*Song of Songs 2:14*

In 1953 Ezio Pinza was singing the love song "Some Enchanted Evening," Kathleen and I were new to public school, and Momma decided to find a husband for our physical education teacher.

Miss Gertrude Thompson would be invited to our home where "across a crowded room"—in this case, across our dining-room table—she would see not one but two strangers. Both men would adore her, as everyone did. She could have her pick.

Best of all, Kathleen and I would get to See It Happen. We'd be the first to tell everyone at school that we'd Been There. In That Room. Where Miss Thompson fell in love. At fifteen and fourteen, Kathleen and I were giddy. This was right out of the movies. Romance! Intrigue! The Surprise of Love!

The cast: Our P.E. teacher, a high-spirited blonde with dimples. All the girls wanted to be like this lively Swedish beauty who'd returned to school in September with a summer tan and hair streaked from sunshine and chlorine. She was fun and funny, so different from the nuns who had taught us before we went to Amos Hiatt Junior High. Except that she was also unmarried, which Momma would remedy.

The two good-looking bachelors were George and Bill, men in their early thirties who roomed at our grandparents' house. Grandma qualified them—as only a landlady can—as hardworking, clean living, and well bred.

The director of this romance, and hostess of the dinner party, said it was best not to inform the cast of the exact nature of the drama that they would enact. Everyone would be too self-conscious, she reasoned.

Momma herself was nervous, as were all of us in on the secret. I don't recall details of the menu or dialogue, but Momma's characteristic habit of peppering everyone with apologetic questions during a meal would no doubt have played out like a 33 record at 78 rpm:

"Is this pot roast stringy?"

"Is this gravy too salty?"

"Is it lumpy?"

Momma liked to call her food by its brand name:

"Don't you want some of this Welch's grape jelly on your corn bread?"

"Would you like a dollop of Kraft Miracle Whip for your Jell-O?"

I imagine that my sisters and dad and I were silent throughout the meal and that the guests provided Momma with a reassuring chorus:

"No, no, it's delicious."

"Everything is wonderful."

"So good."

"Really!"

I'm sure the sterling silver was taken out of its special flannel-lined box and polished: eight place settings with little butter knives, the jelly spoon, the gravy ladle, and the tiny tongs for sugar cubes. My parents' wedding china, made in Japan, had been purchased from a big luxury ship. When we set the table for company, Momma always flicked her fingernail against the rim of an empty goblet, telling us that the clear, musical note was the sound fine crystal made. The stage was carefully set.

Not knowing the ways of public school, it didn't occur to Kathleen or me to wonder if it was unusual for teachers to be invited to a student's home for supper. Nor did we wonder if Bill and George had speculated while driving over about why their landlady's daughter extended a dinner invitation to her parents' roomers, but not to her parents.

We only knew that we were a small part of a grown-up plot, that this was how marriages happened. We understood that the real drama had nothing to do with the questions about whether we wanted Hershey's topping or Planters peanuts or both on our Furnace (the unlikely name of our dairy) ice cream. We knew we were both audience and co-creators of a more exciting romantic mystery than any Hollywood had produced.

Would Miss Thompson pick Bill or George?

Song of Songs is one of Scripture's pure surprises. Pity the scholars whose task it is to explain why this erotic poem is in the Bible. We don't need to worry about why this paean to a lovers' tryst, which offers no lessons in theology or virtue and doesn't even mention God, is in the canon.

Some who insist that the Bible be taken literally—when confronted with this ode to physical human love—suddenly declare the Song an allegory of God's love for Israel or of Christ's love for his Church. We may wonder what they make of the lovers perfuming and grooming themselves to intensify their passions. Of the man's erotic desire for the girl with "breasts . . . like clusters of the vine" and her yearning for a lover who is like "a young stag" (7:9; 8:14). Of the sensual desire behind this invitation to "come to [the] garden and eat its choice fruits" (4:16). Some claim this is an extended "Virgin Mary in union with God" metaphor. Yet this financially independent female lover, the proprietor of her own vineyard, this sexually sophisticated and carnally bold woman is a far cry from the virginal, submissive New Testament Mary.

I'd like to take Song of Songs literally, to say it's in the Bible simply to celebrate human love. Perhaps those who put it in the canon considered the delights of human love—the very surprise of it—sacred. If their reasoning is beyond my understanding, I recognize their placement of the book among the Wisdom Literature as somehow fitting.

The Bible's great stories are full of delightful twists, surprising me at the same time they cause me to exclaim, "But of course!" Helpful strangers turn out to be angelic messengers of God. The Almighty, whose face is often hidden, yearns for human love. Prophets predict what humankind least expects: that power corrupts and contains the seeds of its own destruction even as it flourishes; that I become what I most desire, for good or ill; that only love endures.

Then there is the greatest twist of all: Emmanuel—God-with-us—is not a powerful king or an armor-clad warrior. The incarnation of love is an infant, naked, helpless, born in exile.

George was the lucky man. Two years after the dinner, he and my sister Kathleen became engaged; they married the same month she graduated from high school.

Our children love this story: how all the adults were surprised by love even as they tried to engineer it. We tell them that the difference in George's and Kathleen's ages at the time of the dinner threw all of us off the track: when he fought on Utah Beach in World War II, she'd just entered kindergarten. Our children are surprised that there is a difference in their ages. After forty-three years of marriage, it has long since evaporated.

Bill lived at Grandma's for several years, then eventually moved out to marry. We lost track of him.

Miss Thompson became girls' adviser and assistant principal before she retired. She died of cancer in 1990 at the age of seventy-three, beloved by generations of colleagues and students.

She never married.

My Dearest Maud

*Grandma Maud Miller kept Grandpa waiting
for five long years.*

December 22

My soul doth magnify the Lord. And my spirit hath rejoiced in God my Saviour. For he hath regarded the low estate of his handmaiden: for, behold, from henceforth all generations shall call me blessed.

—Luke 1:46–48 (KJV)

August 12, 1897
Battle Creek

My Dearest Maud:

At Grandmother's I asked [the postman] if he had anything for 29. He had a number of letters, and as soon as I saw one, I did not care what else he had for 29 but took that and [found] some solitary shade, not to weep my sad bosom empty but to fill my sadly empty bosom.

Did I go down the river? Oh! what a question, as though I cared anything about the Kalamazoo River when you are on dry land. No, I stayed at home and thought of you.

That picture of you is too good to be shut out of sight in an old watch case.

With much love,
Your Clyde

August 16, 1897
Battle Creek

My Dearest Maud:

While you are enjoying yourself fishing, be assured I am
not . . . left behind, for yesterday I fished not fish . . . but
clothes. While Father and Mother were gone I did the
washing so that Mother would not have to begin to work as
soon as she came back. I fished the clothes into and out of
the tubs and boiler . . . a string of . . . "fish" 75 ft. long.

The other night I saw Kellogg's house lit up and for a
moment hoped . . . you had come back. But I soon found
out that it was *only* W. K. and son Len and as I [have no]
regard for their health, I did not stop to enquire after it.

When you finish reading this you will wish you hadn't
said anything about that other fellow writing longer letters
to you than I, for I am bound to spoil all his hopes if a long
letter will do it.

With fear and trembling . . . I send my picture West.
Write and tell me what your mother thinks of the Clyde in
the picture.

Oh, Maud, there is but one consolation: the separation
of which you speak *cannot last for all time but must end.*
Five years. It seems a great gulf separating me from all that
life holds dear. With [this] heartache comes the thought
that although I may have said some foolish things, yet much
will be forgiven me by Maud who still loves me [so] I can
face the world and defy it to do its worst. How I wish you
could look beneath this rough old shell and see my heart.

Your Clyde

August 22, 1897
Battle Creek

My Dearest Maud:

Since you have let . . . "One" and "Two" . . . know you do
not care for them anymore, "Number Three" shall keep
[courting you] until he hears orders from headquarters.

Write and tell what an impression I make in the West.
Do not be afraid to tell the truth, for once a dear girl said
something about me that made me resolve she would
change her mind, and I guess I was successful, wasn't I?

"Forewarned is forearmed," yet even if I had four arms
and four legs I would use the latter to run to where you
were and put the former around you.

It is almost time for [brother] Clayton to come home
and . . . I must carry out my threat and make supper. You
see I am cook, washer-woman and house maid combined.
What a treasure I must be.

With all love,
Clyde

September 1, 1897
B.C.

My Dearest Maud:

A girl once *promised* to write *two* letters a week to a boy. She
wrote *one* letter in *two* weeks. Did she keep her promise? If
not why not? This . . . problem caused me many, many
hours of thought, but my stupid old brain could not find
one solution.

Yours with love,
Clyde

February 22, 1898
Battle Creek

My Dearest Maud:

When I came home this evening the snow had to be shoveled away from the barn so I could put the horse out, then the horse had to be unhitched, unharnessed and fed. Next I sold some eggs . . . [Then] it was seven, time to . . . get supper. The stove did nothing but smoke. I stood this half an hour, then . . . took all the wood outdoors, took the stove pipe down, cleaned it, put it back, cleaned the soot from the stove bottom. . . . Now, it is snapping and crackling. . . .Was not your heart affected by my woes of bachelorhood, as in the song, "Moved to Gentle Pity, Yes, Moved to Love"?

Yours,
Clyde

March 27, 1898
B.C.

My Dearest Maud:

Tonight I feel lonesome, what might be called not homesick, but Maudsick, a strong attack.

Write dearest, tell me you love me,
Clyde

September 23, 1899
Milnor, N.D.

Dearest Maud:

I find I have misjudged N.D., for it is not as bad as might
be. Were it not for the blizzards the climate would be
delightful. I went "chicken" hunting with my cousin and
Eld. yesterday afternoon. The dog "flushed" two chickens,
but I had the pleasure of seeing both men waste two shells
apiece and get no chickens.

If I could get a school here and you could get one of the
grades we could get about $100 per mo.

The Scandinavian maidens have no charms for me, dearest, so you need not worry. . . . As I am not attractive, if I
don't make the first advance I am safe.

How much do you love me? Enough to live in N.D.
with me?

Sweetest love from Clyde

October 25, 1899
Milnor, N.D.

Dearest Maud:

No, I have not forgotten: Send me the measure of your finger
and as soon as I get to Minneapolis or any city I will keep my
promise. Of course it is not wrong for you to want a ring. I
have been careless to not act on it before, but I always said,
"Maud and I know how much we love one another, and that
is all that is needed." But I know how you feel dearest, and I
shall get you something to remember me by.

Good night, darling,
Clyde

January 8, 1900
De Lamere, N.D.

My Dearest Maud:

About the ring: of course I will not be offended, for had it weighed a 1,000 lbs it would not have been too good for you. It seemed to be rather heavy, but . . . most of the rings I have seen are as heavy, if not heavier.

You might suggest to the fellows of Davis City, [Iowa], to Doc in particular, that if they are so deeply worried over you I can make it a point to come and give them 5 ft 11-1/2 in. of explanation [with] full and explicit directions for over-coming their "aching void."

Without you the struggle would be long and hopeless.

Love, kisses and tender thoughts, from Clyde

January 16, 1900
De Lamere, N.D.

My Dearest Maud:

All aboard for your questions: De Lamere is a place as would make a dog homesick for a good colony of fleas, so that he might have something to be interested in. The Scandinavians [are not] too sociable. They seldom hire teachers here til obliged to. . . . The principal aims to get somebody to pay him for the privilege of teaching.

You must not become discouraged on account of the way I write about N.D., for it is better to plan on little, then if we get a good deal we are happily surprised. All I desire, dearest, is enough for comfort and a trifle to lay by for a rainy day.

The only drawback I think of is what if I have not pre-pared . . . to earn a livelihood. Were I certain of $500 yearly income . . . I would not stop a moment. . . . I do not love you less because I calculate the cost, but more rather, that I try to keep you from . . . needless hardships. If I had any other way of making a living. . . . Alas! darling. I am not gifted and although there [is work I could do] on the Sabbath . . . I cannot silence conscience. . . .

Be brave. The future looks hopeful. I am happy to know you are pleased with your ring.

Love, kisses, from Clyde

January 22, 1900
De Lamere

My Dearest:

My school . . . is in bad shape. The last teacher was nothing extra, and the pupils got to doing as they pleased, and the parents do not . . . [make] them mind. I am getting them straightened out. . . .

Oh! that I only knew more so I could earn more, and have you with me. That you have made a bad bargain in getting me will not be excuse enough to make me let you go.

To the sweetest, dearest, purest girl in the world,
from your Clyde

February 12, 1900
De Lamere

My Dearest Maud:

I have at times thought you were foolish about E. G. Norman, but dearest, loving me as you do and not knowing that E. G. had given up the struggle *I do not blame you, no,*

I love you the more for your fears, for they simply show that my love meant all to you. So remember, darling, that whatever you see fit to do in the Norman matter, Clyde trusts you.

I do not want to spend another winter in N.D., or anywhere else, alone.

Love, kisses and all my heart,
Clyde

March 7, 1900
De Lamere, N.D.

My Dearest Maud:

My N.D. prospects are dead. My cousin expects to run for [superintendent's office] and Simpson takes it out on me.

You need not worry about Clyde thinking you were not doing right by not shutting yourself away from the young people. Let people think what they wish, Clyde knows you are the truest girl in this whole world. You must not [forgo] amusement. Of course, I do not care about going out in society, but . . . I have my school work to interest me.

We will show people whether I am out in the cold or not. There will be a few surprised persons in D.C. when they find out Maud loves me more than anyone else.

Although the future looks dark, I shall keep on hoping [to] have you, if you will but wait.

Love to Maud, my Maud, from Clyde

April 11, 1900
Montrose, Minnesota

My Dearest Maud:

Tomorrow I talk with the Board. I think I can get $40/mo.
I should have liked a better paying position but this is better
than nothing. . . .

I guess the [Iowans] do not know my girl or they would
never think the "Miller fellow" was not in it. We will show
them, won't we dearest?

Ten thousand kisses to Maud, from her Clyde

*Mary and Maud are called to adventure, and like the clas-
sic heroes, they at first resist the call.*

*"But how can this be?" Mary protests. "For I do not know
a man."*

*We don't have Maud's letters, but she seems to be writing,
"Let's wait five years, Clyde. I'm having too much fun now."*

*Maud is easier to understand than Mary, at least than the
fearful, ever-obedient Virgin Mother, conceived and conceiving
without sin.*

*Centuries of celibate men fixate on Mary's gynecology, por-
traying her as sexless and perfect. As if a fully human woman
must be a Jezebel, a "devil's food" cupcake enticing mortals to
gluttony. Chocolate, though, is satanic only to the dieter; God
blesses the fruits of his creation and calls them good.*

*We who needn't fret about dogma don't care if you're
a virgin, Mary. We don't care if Jesus is "illegitimate"—it makes
us laugh to think he may have embodied his message that perfectly. We're puzzled by men who revere you as the mother who
teaches Jesus compassion, mercy, and love but would deny you his
priesthood; who sentimentalize you at the stable and at the foot
of the cross but would ban you from his altar; who venerate you*

holding your dead son, weeping, but would forbid you to raise his chalice and say, "Remember."

Mary, we hardly know you! Have I been too literal, too obsessed with your body to grasp your spirit? Too angry not to relish a battle of the sexes for ownership of you? Too privileged to long for the feminine face of God?

Do only the oppressed understand your radical praise of a God who has "dispersed the arrogant . . . thrown down the rulers . . . but lifted up the lowly" (Luke 1:51–52)? Do only the downtrodden see you clearly—as the olive-skinned Madonna of Guadalupe, the red-skinned Cherokee Madonna, the Black Madonna of the Disappeared of Latin America, or of Czestochowa, expressing the Polish people's yearning for freedom? You appear in apparitions to peasant women and children, leading them to defy popes and bishops and entrusting them with secrets withheld from the powerful.

Theologians and other sophisticates are embarrassed by visions that sustain oppressed people or cause them to be brave. But those of low estate see you as strong because you have the guts to make God human; because you question angels and ponder things in your heart; because you witness your son's death; because your Lord scatters "the arrogant of mind and heart" and fills the hungry "with good things" (Luke 1:51, 53). Such a God-bearer does magnify the divine, and humanity too: for unto us a child is born.

Maud is not so quick to say yes. Why doesn't she alleviate Clyde's long misery? Does the memory of her own awful homesickness—in the Kellogg Sanitarium with TB—make her fear leaving home again? Does Maud see marriage and children as a call to adventure or as a call to sorrow? (Or does she already suspect it is both?)

Go for it, Grandma. Write Clyde yes. W. K. Kellogg will give him a job, and Clyde will hate it. He'll take you out to Montana—Indian territory—and you'll make him bring you back home to Iowa, just like your "difficult" mother Abigail did. Then, surprise! Your parents will leave again, to find their Promised Land in California.

It doesn't matter. When you say yes, you cross the threshold of your own great adventure. So say yes to your hopes and fears, and we'll go "over the river and through the woods to Grandmother's house" for our most cherished Christmases. Say yes, Grandma, and all our generations shall call you blessed.

April 24, 1911
C. H. Miller
Attorney-at-Law
409-11 D. M. Life Bldg.
Des Moines, Iowa

My Dear Wife and Babies:

It is late, but I must . . . write so you will know you are missed back here in Iowa. Am still far under the work, but as [the stenographer] is breaking in, I see light ahead.

If you were to drop in as a surprise, you would want to drop back after one look at the house. The electricians finished this noon, and the lathers should be through tonight, then comes the plasterers, after which comes the carpenters, followed by the paper hanger and painter, following closely comes the job of cleaning up, while last but not least comes the *bills.*

I love you. . . . Kiss the "bunnies" for me, and imagine you are getting one from me.

With love as ever,
Your "hubby" Clyde.

Peanuts and Pops, Moses, David, and Paul

A.D. 1874

One of the few big city churches marked by mob legend
is Chicago's Holy Name Cathedral. As the story goes,
stray bullets hit the church's cornerstone when Al Capone's
hit man gunned down Hymie Weiss in what is now the
church's parking lot.

DECEMBER 23

But who will endure the day of his coming?
And who can stand when he appears?
                                        —*Malachi 3:2*

When I moved to Chicago in the late seventies, I learned that the city still enjoys its Al Capone image. I met and married Stanford, a Windy City native who—like all Chicagoans—had absorbed gangster lore. A onetime University of Chicago English major, Stan can identify characters like Murray "the Camel" Humphrey and "Greasy Thumb" Guzik as easily as Leopold Bloom, Madame Bovary, and Huck Finn.

Stan's dad had told his boys he'd "won the war with a typewriter," referring to his many World War I Atlantic crossings as a navy yeoman clerk-typist. Since "typewriter" was mob slang for "machine gun," Stan's childhood image of that service record was not what his father had intended.

I listened to such stories as an outsider, but I soon learned that you can't live in Chicago long without running into a gangster.

I was driving Stan's car, with my son Brian, then sixteen, in the passenger seat. Brian had made flower boxes, and we were looking for a place that sold petunias. Craning my neck to see the addresses on Ashland Avenue, I failed to look at the road.

Suddenly a clamor of noise and turbulence pitched us violently forward, then slammed us back. We had plowed into the trunk of a parked car.

"Are you okay, Mom?" Brian asked.

I looked over at him. "Your head." His curly brown hair was powdered with slivers of glass, like angel dust on a Christmas tree. His head had punched a concave dent in the windshield, splintering it into a glass spiderweb.

I hadn't anticipated the crash, so I hadn't braked. I'd rammed into the trunk of a pink Cadillac that was double-parked in our lane. An ox of a man tramped out of a store to gape at his car's rear end, which was compacted like a stomped-on beer can. The thick-necked man turned away from the pile of pink rubbish that had been his Cadillac, pushed through a crowd of bystanders, and filled my driver's-side window with his jowly face.

"You didn't see my car, lady?" Amazed, stupefied, not angry.

I shook my head. How otherwise to explain a full-force thirty-five-mile-per-hour collision with no skid marks on the street?

"Ya got insurance, doncha?" the face asked.

Still stunned, I equated "insurance" with "health" because I was a freelancer always worried about medical coverage. I said no, unaware he meant auto insurance. He stomped away, shaking his head, then swiveled and came back.

"Look, ma'am, I got insurance. We'll work it out. Just between us. Don't get the police involved. Okay?" I nodded, agreeing to whatever he said. But the accident was big enough that bystanders had already called the cops, so I got a ticket for hitting a parked car.

On the way to the hospital, I looked back to see the pink car dangling from a tow-truck hook like a snared salmon, dripping fluids.

Stan and his brother rushed to the ER and found us okay. While we waited for Brian's head to be bandaged, Stan and Dick studied my traffic ticket for information about the collision. Dick pointed to my victim's name: Mr. Paul Panczko, the Cadillac owner. Their hushed exchange followed:

"Do you think?"

"Is he out?"

"It's gotta be."

"Peanuts Panczko."

Stan told me I'd run smack into organized crime.

Peanuts, the son of Polish immigrants, was the youngest and boldest Panczko. He and two burglar brothers, Pops and Butch, were known for audacious capers.

Chicago reporters loved the Panczko brothers, whose early specialty as jewelry thieves yielded great copy. The brothers would follow a traveling salesman's car, eyeing the sample case of gems in his trunk. One would call the police in the salesman's state, claiming to be a Chicago cop needing a license check to get the name of the car's owner. Then he'd call the car dealer, claiming to be a locksmith. "This guy's locked his keys in the car," Pops would say. "I need the serial number to make a duplicate." When the salesman stopped for dinner, they'd unlock the trunk and take the samples. The salesman would be hours and miles away before he'd discover the jewels were gone. The boys conned cops and car dealers for years.

Pops was the likable buffoon. Tired of being constantly tailed by the police, he once jumped onto the back of a produce truck and started bouncing onions off of the cops' windshield.

Pops was charged with attempting to hijack a truckload of onions, but the case was thrown out of court when the trucker couldn't identify the evidence as his onions. Their lawyer, Georgie Bieber, was good.

Bieber claimed he represented the Panczkos at no charge; he got paid in free publicity. Bieber charged plenty, but he didn't run the money through his firm or pay taxes on it. In Chicago, everyone was on the take. The Panczkos learned from the papers that their victims exaggerated losses in order to steal from the insurance companies. The brothers bribed cops, judges, parole officers, and, it was rumored, jurors. With all the payoffs, the Panczkos complained they hardly had time to steal for themselves.

The boys had a social conscience, though it operated selectively. After they discovered a cocker spaniel in a car they stole, they were moved by the owner's pleas for his dog's return. Pops called the victim to direct him to the synagogue yard where he'd tied the pooch. When they robbed a Brink's truck at its last pickup at Divine Savior Catholic Church, the boys left the Sunday collections behind.

Peanuts was slicker than Pops. It was the difference between onions and karats. Peanuts scored big and gambled it away. He made *The Guinness Book of World Records* for pulling the biggest jewel robbery in U.S. history, down in Pompano Beach. His gang was caught red-handed due to a series of blunders involving a boat that wouldn't start. Luck and Bieber were with him. Peanuts never spent a day in jail for this historic heist in spite of getting a life sentence. Trials, mistrials, endless appeals, two hung juries, and rumors of a Chicago-style fix were slow death to the prosecution.

If God is coming to judge us, who can stand before him? Malachi asks. This prophet's strongest criticism is for the religious—priests who betray their calling. Those in positions of trust—police, judges, teachers, parents, me—sin more grievously when we betray than do criminals.

God is weary of hearing "Why aren't you just?" from those who don't ask that question of themselves, Malachi says. God wants to know: "Why aren't you *just?" Quit separating the world into "law-abiding, good folk like me" and felons.*

Let's not sentimentalize Peanuts Panczko. Unlike Pops, he carried guns when he worked. A life of crime is not all laughs: Peanuts and Pops were often beaten unconscious by police officers. When everyone's on the take, everyone gets brutal. Evil isn't always entertaining copy.

Does even God have a shadow side? Didn't the Creator of All create the serpent too? Does the entwining of good and evil in every being and every thing constitute life's essential struggle? Why did an all-merciful God permit unspeakable atrocities in Auschwitz and Cambodia? Why did all of Christendom? Can I, who didn't suffer there, presume to answer these questions?

"Remember the law of Moses," Malachi warns (3:22). Remember also that Moses was a murderer, as were David and Paul. Born selfish, I'm intrigued by evil too. If put to the test, I suspect I'm capable of what I most deplore. When and if the Spirit lives in me, it's not because I lack a dark side but because I am so much in need of Grace.

I collided with Peanuts during his time between stints of hard time; he spent more than twenty-six years in jail. Bieber reduced sixty-odd arrests to only three convictions. One was when cops found Peanuts carrying keys to every Chicago postal box, a federal offense if you're not a postal employee.

Peanuts called several times, assuring me that we could "settle this just between us." I wondered what was in that car trunk I'd pleated into a pink-metal accordion. He lived nearby, in my Wrigley Field neighborhood, over on the lakefront.

"The important thing is that your boy is okay," he'd say, always friendly, neighborly, one parent to another. He had a daughter. Stan warned, "Don't talk to him. Refer him to my office. Our insurance will take care of it."

Shortly after our crash, Peanuts vanished into the Federal Witness Protection Program. He sometimes appears in Quantico to lecture to FBI recruits. Pops, too, became a better citizen in his old age, advising homeowners on burglar-proofing their houses and telling kids to avoid crime. He's been a guest speaker at a Chicago Crime Commission luncheon and at the Merry Gangsters Literary Society.

I became one of those gangster-savvy Chicagoans. When Brian went away to college, I sent him newspaper clippings of the Panczko boys' latest capers. Peanuts had become "our" mobster. I learned that the Panczko parents had lived in Chicago's Bad Lands, a dangerous, poverty-stricken area, in the era before welfare assistance. Peanuts, Pops, and Butch had started young; for them it was steal food or starve— daily—since the family couldn't afford a refrigerator. They'd had no toilet, no running water. No birthdays had been marked; Santa had never visited.

Three other siblings had led clean lives, and I couldn't say which way out I'd have chosen under similar conditions, when even law-enforcement officials were models of corruption. "There but for the grace of God, go I," I think, disturbed only when I recall Peanuts' final transgression.

In exchange for leniency, he gave the FBI evidence to convict his colleagues. Pops was one of those he handed over.

That Great Cloud of Witnesses

On a cloudy day I can almost see all those big-footed Graneys and talkative Millers and flat-fannied Topliffs who've gone on before us.

CHRISTMAS VIGIL

❧❦❧

*The book of the genealogy of Jesus Christ, the son of David,
the son of Abraham. Abraham became the father of Isaac,
Isaac the father of Jacob.*

—Matthew 1:1–2

The communion of saints is a rare incident of warmhearted dogma. I first embraced it in ninth grade after I came home from school one day and Momma told me, "Sharon's father has died. Go change clothes and I'll take you over. I've talked to her mother, and they'd like us to come."

I sat in the bathtub, barely able to comprehend what I'd heard. I was much older before I realized how young my best friend's father was—thirty-six. Then I only thought of him as a dad, a former navy barber who cut his only child's hair. I'd never heard of a girl my age losing a parent to a sudden heart attack, without any warning. It felt odd to be changing into my dressy Sunday navy blue dress to go see Sharon.

When we arrived, her mother's sister and brother-in-law were there. Sharon was in the basement playing the piano. I went downstairs and asked her if she wanted to spend the night, told her I had pictures from our week at Lake Okoboji. Her mother encouraged her to come with us. Our family went out to eat at a nice restaurant, Johnny and Kay's, out by the airport. Treating this evening as a special event was the only indication of what had happened. No one mentioned the death until Sharon came up to my bedroom and I closed the door.

"I don't know what will become of us," Sharon said, wondering how she and her mother would get along. She told me of the rush to the hospital, how she and her mom waited a long time until a nurse came to say she was so sorry and ask if Sharon would like to lie down. Someone called her aunt and uncle, the only relatives in town. Then they went home without her father.

Sometime during that long, sad day, Sharon's mother told her, "You don't have to sit here. Is there anything you'd like to do?" "I wanted to play the piano," Sharon said, shrugging, not understanding anything of that day, including herself. She sat down in the basement alone, playing the piano, until I came.

That was when I began to pray for "the repose of his soul," without understanding what that meant, and for Sharon and for myself as well. Seeing how death had devastated a family, I wanted us all to rest in peace.

Over the years since then, I've added names to the list of dead I invoke and commemorate: grandparents and great-grandparents, in-laws and steps, aunts, uncles, cousins, friends, teachers, colleagues. The AIDS victims on my list include people I didn't know who were dear to those I do. Sharon and I lost touch after high school, but every roll call still begins with her father, that first death in 1952 when we were fourteen.

My communion is primarily with those I knew and loved, but that great cloud of witnesses expands in my understanding to encompass all the patriarchs and matriarchs of faith and family: Abraham, Elijah, John the Baptist, Mary, Saints Dismas and Rocco, Rabbis Nahum and Yehuda ha-Nassi, all the big-footed Graneys and talkative Millers and flat-fannied Topliffs I knew, and those who preceded them.

This involves much more than honoring and preserving their memory, though it does that. Prayerfully invoking their names gives witness to my connectedness with them and, through them, to the high courts of infinity and Spirit. It leads me to appreciate how my relationship with those who preceded me in death is ongoing, mutually blessed, sometimes deeper and richer now than it was in life. This reciprocity is richly mysterious: in ways I can't understand, my prayers benefit them; they intercede somehow or other on my behalf.

I am encouraged by participating in a dimension greater than the blip on the calendar that is my life. The communion of living and dead that I know, knew, have yet to meet, and never will encounter—we—constitute the first word of the Lord's Prayer: "our."

Sometime beyond time, maybe I'll see and be with them all: Horencio Gulia and Padre Pio, the angel Gabriel and Miss Thompson, Abraham Lincoln and Peanuts Panczko, Aunt Harriett and Arthur Murray, Sister Aggie and Sister Ellen White, Babe Didrickson Zaharias and JFK, Harry Truman and Nikita Khrushchev, Saint Nick and Sarah Nass, Nurse Potter and W. K. Kellogg, Jesse Elsworth and the old man who pinched Momma in the movie, those I have wronged, fought with, forgiven, and forgotten, and men and women and children who have yet to appear to complicate and grace my life.

Matthew's genealogy establishes that Joseph descended from David so that the adopted child Jesus can claim his father's royal lineage. Only the father's heritage is important to those who record the Bible's "begats."

So why do a few women appear on this patriarchal record, including some of questionable reputation (Tamar, Rahab) along with Ruth, the wife of Uriah, and Mary? Perhaps the fame of each woman tempts Matthew to remind his readers of her link to the husband and son. The men are identified by their relationship to the women.

Why does Luke's genealogy differ from Matthew's? Perhaps because, truth to tell, all those branches of family trees are less important than our common roots. Blood and legal ties do not matter as much as an intimate association with and the influence of godly persons. Justice and charity cultivated become dominant traits, and virtue is passed to the next generation as surely as brown eyes. Strongly held values of ancestors (ones we knew and ones we didn't) outlive them to be remembered by subsequent generations in family codes and conduct. Ancient family lessons become flags of recognition or warning: sibling loyalty or betrayal; obsessions with justice or revenge; an affinity for the underdog or for the worst of the opposite sex; huge investments in time, resources, work, or family.

Individual and historic turning points are recognized in hindsight. Looking back, one sees how a prophet, plague, invention, marriage, or disaster led to a new era. Only the artificial turning points of a calendar are ones we anticipate: new decades, anniversaries, a bicentennial.

We are among the relatively few in history who have lived to usher in a new millennium, a universally awe-inspiring passage, another thousand years since the birth of one child. In the blink of an eye that was his thirty years on earth, his life split recorded time into "before" and "after."

This fully human revelation of the Divine pitched his tent among us, and ever since, humankind has probed his meaning, seeking to inherit his Spirit. The urgency to claim him honors him with heroism and service to the stranger, the needy, the imprisoned and violates him with hatred and war. Such an anniversary calls for looking backward and forward, elicits hopes and fears, prompts plans for jubilee and apocalypse. Should I celebrate or repent? Probably both.

Family stories put flesh on the bones of genealogy charts and are more useful. While all our family members don't inhabit the same gene pool, we inhabit each other's stories.

What are the lessons of all this history? What could I say to my descendants more than a hundred years from now, those twenty-second-century pioneers of the new millennium? Something like this:

When you feel most at home, you may be at the very beginning of your journey. You may seek a new place, or you may stay and entertain angels, right where you are. Either choice requires courage and fortitude.

Laughter helps.

Stories recalled in family dairies, letters, and in the telling by one generation to the next speak powerfully to those who hear them. They enhance and illuminate the ancient Judeo-Christian tales. All are sacred.

Listen.

Save your love letters. Trash your journals and any self-indulgent accounts of your passions and politics, the uncensored scorecards of your victories and defeats. The love letters will document your truth.

Be thankful.

Cherish surprises: the kindness of strangers, the phone call that changes your life, the event that forces strength you didn't know you possessed. What comes out of left field can set you in the right direction.

Pay attention.

Your story isn't finished yet. When loss or failure overwhelms you, think of how you and your descendants may view this moment ten, fifty, and one hundred years from now.

If you don't circle around your disappointments endlessly, they hone your navigating skills.

Keep trying.

A writer once said all stories are the story of Job, of trying to find God's face in suffering. He overlooked Mrs. Job's story: the overburdened caretaker who also loses everything, the helpless witness to her loved one's anguish. No one questions her suffering to give it significance or even asks how she's holding up. Her story is yours when all that's left of better days is your justifiable terror of ever loving again.

Love anyway.

On a shrinking planet, anger and pride require smaller houses than forbearance and humility.

Forgive.

Ordinary people relying on Infinite Goodness and Promises have overcome oppression without violence.

Seek peace.

How you design, fall into, or inherit a family is not important; how you honor it is. In all final judgments—including your own—you receive not the benefits of your labor and your learning but the bounty of your love.

Remember.

The Most Familiar Surprise

*Grandma Miller with Gerald, who died at age twelve
but still lives in our family stories.*

CHRISTMAS MASS AT MIDNIGHT

*And it came to pass in those days, that there went out a
decree from Caesar Augustus, that all the world should
be taxed.*

—Luke 2:1 (KJV)

We chose an 8:30 P.M. Christmas Eve service at a Florida
Lutheran church we had no links to because it suited
our bedtimes and complex family schedule. We also hoped
our kids would sit still for the children's reenactment of the
Nativity.

At the back of the busy church, people wished each other
merry Christmas, little angels got their halos positioned,
greeters gave us candles, and teenagers offered child care for
our three-year-old. We'd come in two cars and didn't end up
sitting in the same pew; it seemed a miracle we'd made it at
all amidst the airport pickups, shopping, trimming, wrapping, thawing, peeling, and baking we'd immersed ourselves
in. It was a relief to sit down and draw a breath.

A piano refrain signaled eight elderly women in choir
robes to begin a quavery "Silent Night."

Someone announced the name of the family who would portray Mary, Joseph, and the Christ child, an honor that goes every year to the newest member of the congregation. Tonight's honoree was only three days old.

As the pastor read the words "because there was no room for them in the inn," the couple brought their newborn to the manger at the front of the altar. The mother didn't actually place the baby in the manger, but held him instead. I understood she wanted to prevent the baby from crying during the pageant. I sympathized, but part of me hoped the baby would make some minor noises, just to reinforce the point of the story.

The catch in my throat came when the pastor said, "And there were in the same country shepherds abiding in the field." He hesitated, having given the cue, and looked to the vestibule to find the actors.

Young shepherds burst down the aisle—rubber thongs slapping the floor, the cloths tied around their heads askew—to kneel in place, breathless, before the child. Once when I was their age—acting in just such a pageant—I suddenly understood: this is Christmas. Not Santa or Rudolph or Frosty or all those others who feed on the story, but this account of the birth of a child.

"For unto you is born this day in the city of David a Saviour." A flock of young angels fluttered down the aisle, white gowned, winged, haloed with tinsel, bringing us tidings of great joy.

Then came three solemn kings, turbaned, with fake black beards, holding glittery offerings.

The lights dimmed and a piano began the familiar strains of "O Little Town of Bethlehem." One candle tilted towards another and then another, spreading the power of light in the hushed darkness. The fragile choir voices were boosted by our own, until the church was aglow with the glorious harmony of peace on earth for that one sacred moment:

> Where children pure and happy
> Pray to the blessed Child
> Where misery cries out to Thee,
> Son of the mother mild;
> Where charity stands watching
> And faith holds wide the door,
> The dark night wakes, the glory breaks,
> And Christmas comes once more.

The ancient story begins anew. Caesar orders the census; Cyrenius governs Syria. It is a world of patronage and powerful men, of people who work the land and the sea, of those who trade goods and collect taxes, of teachers, magicians, healers, prophets, bandits, harlots, lepers, demons, and angels. It is reasonable to bring certain assumptions to a story set in this time and place. I pay attention, knowing they're going to be shaken:

Herod dominates life on earth. What he commands will be done. If there were ever to be a person mightier than Herod, he would have to be a rich and powerful king with a tremendous army.

The wise men glean wisdom from the stars but—knowing where the real power lies—will do Herod's bidding.

Zechariah's wife, Elizabeth, is barren, too old to have a child.

Joseph and Mary, a laborer and his betrothed, are nothing out of the ordinary. Their hometown, Nazareth, is an unimpressive little burg inhabited by hicks.

I hope to be excited, amazed, stretched, to transcend my world and time. I like that this story is two thousand years old, that I know it so well I don't have to hear it again. But of course I do.

It ends with that greatest and most familiar surprise: a baby. A vulnerable infant mightier than kings and armies. The child is born though powerful forces try to kill him, though there is no place for him in the hearts or homes of this world. Love triumphs over evil, indifference, doubt—all the attempts of the universe to thwart it.

God's grace is a Somebody.

*A*nd all went to be taxed, every one into his own city. And Joseph also went up from Galilee, out of the city of Nazareth, into Judaea, unto the city of David, which is called Bethlehem; (because he was of the house and lineage of David:) To be taxed with Mary his espoused wife, being great with child. And so it was, that, while they were there, the days were accomplished that she should be delivered. And she brought forth her firstborn son, and wrapped him in swaddling clothes, and laid him in a manger; because there was no room for them in the inn. And there were in the same country shepherds abiding in the field, keeping watch over their flock by night. And, lo, the angel of the Lord came upon them, and the glory of the Lord shone round about them: and they were sore afraid. And the angel said unto them, Fear not: for, behold, I bring you good tidings of great joy, which shall be to all people. For unto you is born this day in the city of David a Saviour, which is Christ the Lord. And this shall be a sign unto you; Ye shall find the babe wrapped in swaddling clothes, lying in a manger. And suddenly there was with the angel a multitude of the heavenly host praising God, and saying, Glory to God in the highest, and on earth peace, good will toward men.

—Luke 2:3–14 (KJV)

Sources

Among Bible translations, I have most often used the New American Bible. In a few instances, other versions seemed truer to the spirit of my story or purpose. A few favorite verses cried for the magnificent language of the King James Version (the Nativity, in Luke 2:1–14 and the Magnificat of Luke 1:46). I also cite Father Daniel Berrigan's translation in *Isaiah: Spirit of Courage, Gift of Tears* (Minneapolis, Minn.: Fortress Press, 1996) and the Revised Standard Version. Everett Fox's insightful *Five Books of Moses* (New York: Schocken Books, 1995) was referred to often though not used for any specific passage, and I also benefited from the insights of contemporary translators Eugene Peterson, for *The Message: Psalms* (Colorado Springs, Colo.: NavPress, 1994), and Reynolds Price, for *Three Gospels* (New York: Scribner, 1996).

I am indebted to the following for anecdotes used in this book:

Baumann, Ed, and John O'Brien. *Polish Robbin' Hoods: The Inside Story of the Panczko Brothers.* Chicago: Bonus Books, 1992.

Delaney, John J. *Dictionary of Saints.* New York: Doubleday, 1980.

Dubos, Rene. *The White Plague: Tuberculosis, Man, and Society.* New Brunswick, N.J.: Rutgers University Press, 1987.

Gilmour, Peter. "St. Joseph Gets Buried in His Work." *U.S. Catholic,* March 1998.

Gould, Tony. *A Summer Plague: Polio and Its Survivors.* New Haven, Conn.: Yale University Press, 1995.

Grossman, Ron. "Breakfast Serial." *Chicago Tribune,* 6 March 1992.

Halpin, Anne. *The Naming of Flowers.* New York: Harper and Row, 1990.

Khrushchev, Nikita. *Khrushchev Remembers.* Translated by Strobe Talbott. Boston: Little, Brown, 1974.

King, Martin Luther, Jr. "I See the Promised Land." In *A Testament of Hope: The Essential Writings of Martin Luther King, Jr.,* edited by James Melvin Washington. New York: Harper and Row, 1986.

Lerman, Liz. "Are Miracles Enough? Thoughts on Time, Transformation, and the Meaning of Community." *Dance/USA Journal,* spring 1993.

Reynolds, Quentin. "The Girl Who Lived Again." *Reader's Digest,* October 1954.

Salerno, Jeanette. "All That You Can Imagine Is Not All That There Is." *The Voice of Padre Pio,* summer 1993, 181.

Shipler, David K. *Russia: Broken Idols, Solemn Dreams.* New York: Times Books, 1983.

Treves, Sir Frederick. "Autobiography of the Elephant Man." In *The True History of the Elephant Man,* edited by Michael Howell and Peter Ford. London: Allison and Busby, 1980.

Walesa, Lech. *The Struggle and the Triumph.* New York: Arcade Publishing, 1991.

Wiesel, Elie. "Elijah." In *Five Biblical Portraits.* Notre Dame, Ind.: University of Notre Dame Press, 1981.